'Jessie Cole is peerless in Australian letters; for me,
she is the master chronicler of hidden psychic spaces.
Her exquisite new memoir compels, startles and
affirms the arterial centre that is desire.'
ELLENA SAVAGE, author of *Blueberries*

'A gorgeous journey of a writer seeking out the inaccessible
part of herself, of those she loves, and who love her back, and
of the forest that holds them all together. *Desire* is a book of
intellectual and emotional depth, exploring the flesh and nerves
and sinew — as a mother, a lover, a friend and soothsayer. A
tender joy of a book, about life and death, and of all the great
pulls in between. Raw and fascinating writing that shimmers
with truth and beauty at once. A confession, a lament,
a celebration — I cannot recommend this enough.'
TARA JUNE WINCH, author of *The Yield*

'Jessie Cole is a delight. I don't know how she does it. She drags
the gnarliest anchors from the heaviest depths and throws light
on the hardest of places — her prose shimmers with warmth
and breathtaking honesty. *Desire* is about the mystery of our
bodies, how the wiring can get crossed, connections lost and
one woman's delicate unstitching to find herself.'
ANNA KRIEN, *author of Night Games*

DESIRE

Jessie Cole is a writer. Her first novel, *Darkness on the Edge of Town*, was shortlisted for the 2013 ALS Gold Medal and longlisted for the Dobbie Literary Award. Her second novel, *Deeper Water*, was released in 2014 to critical acclaim. *Staying*, a memoir, was longlisted for the 2019 Colin Roderick Award and shortlisted for the Victorian Premier's Literary Award for Non-Fiction. She lives in northern New South Wales.

jessie-cole.com

Desire

A Reckoning

Jessie Cole

TEXT PUBLISHING MELBOURNE AUSTRALIA

The Text Publishing Company acknowledges the Traditional Owners of the country on which we work, the Wurundjeri people of the Kulin Nation, and pays respect to their Elders past and present.

textpublishing.com.au

The Text Publishing Company
Wurundjeri Country, Level 6, Royal Bank Chambers, 287 Collins Street, Melbourne Victoria 3000 Australia

Published by The Text Publishing Company, 2022

Cover design by Jessica Horrocks
Page design by Text
Cover image based on illustration by Kristina Balashova / Stocksy
Typeset by J&M Typesetting

Printed and bound in Australia by Griffin Press, part of Ovato, an accredited ISO/NZS 14001:2004 Environmental Management System printer.

ISBN: 9781922458667 (paperback)
ISBN: 9781922459954 (ebook)

A catalogue record for this book is available from the National Library of Australia.

This book was written on the traditional lands of the Moorung-moobah people of the Bundjalung Nation. The author acknowledges the Traditional Owners of the land on which she works, and pays respects to Indigenous Elders past, present and emerging. As the traditional custodians of these lands, the Moorung-moobah people have lived in and derived their physical and spiritual needs from the forests, rivers, lakes and streams of this beautiful valley over many thousands of years. Sovereignty has never been ceded.

For the forest and all my forest kin

contents

~

fireflies

At dusk, in springtime, there is a stretch of trees in my homeplace where the fireflies sometimes hover. I might walk there, by chance, at just the right time. Caught in this rare moment, standing amongst them, I'm awed by their tiny luminescent bodies. Each creature's light is intermittent, blinking, so I lose sight of them for several beats, only to have them reappear beside me, slightly out of place. Keeping still, the night darkening around me, the light of the fireflies invisible then not, invisible then not, I try to hold the moment, wishing time would stop.

The first night I spent with my lover was like standing amongst the fireflies. Desire incandescent, but the knowledge of its fleetingness always in the room. I thought, I may never see this man again. I thought, the memory may be all that remains. And I tried not to let that knowledge change me. I tried not to pre-emptively grieve. Be here now, I told myself. Be here now.

understorey

Some days, especially when I'm away from my forest homeplace, I stumble around, bumping and bruising myself, taking off skin. I can't gauge where my body is in space. I can't feel my edges. I feel pain when I come up against a hard object, but I'm shocked by the pain, surprised that my body has come a cropper. The supermarket trolley jerks against my ankles. My elbows bang against walls as I walk past. Hallways don't seem to contain me. I ricochet from one knock to another, bump bump bump. It all seems like extreme clumsiness, but I wasn't a clumsy child. I can't bring any sense of self — the boundary lines of my body — with me from the forest out into the world.

~

What to do with the intensity of longing that occasionally arises? Sometimes I hug my pup so hard he growls. When my pup growls, I realise I need to find some other way of letting off steam. It's easy to imagine I could just touch myself and be done with it, but no matter how many times I make myself come, that feeling of wanting doesn't subside. A friend has a term for the need for touch — 'skin-hungry'. Lots of people live without sex, but I find it a kind of deprivation.

~

My local vet is preposterously handsome. Dark-skinned, almond-eyed, of indeterminate (to me) ethnicity, youthful. When I first walked into his surgery with my scab-nosed cat, I sucked in a breath in surprise. He smirked, as if his appeal was written all over my face. The last vet was an old, gentle, dishevelled bloke, who wiped up the urine of nervous pets as if it was nothing. This new young vet had the cocky ease of someone aware of their charms. I wondered about how he'd see me. I lived in a house with few mirrors, days might go past before I caught sight of my reflection. Self-conscious, I glanced down at my tatty jeans, untying my messy hair while he spoke. I pondered our age difference. I guessed it was about a decade. I wondered if he'd see me as old. There was something in his manner that hinted at an awareness of me as a sexual being. Was he flirting with me? Or did I imagine that because I found him attractive? The sexual undercurrent caught me off guard. I tied my hair back up, alert, my body tingling. He stared into my eyes and told me he suspected my scab-nosed cat was allergic to mosquitos, but that I'd have to pay six hundred dollars for a biopsy to check.

I did not have six hundred dollars.

'But how would you treat it, if it was mosquitos?'

The old vet had always prescribed the cheapest possible option.

'Well, there is a range of potential treatments, but I'm not willing to go ahead with any of them until we know what we're dealing with.'

'Can't we just assume it is mosquitos, and give the simplest treatment a go?' It was tricky to broach the topic of my limited income.

He shook his head.

I sighed in frustration.

'Have you thought about getting pet insurance?' he asked. 'I mean, you wouldn't go without car insurance, right? It's pretty much the same.'

I'd only ever had third-party car insurance.

I'm a single mum, I wanted to say. Or, even more financially damning, I'm a fucking novelist.

I did what any desperate owner of a scab-nosed cat would do in this scenario. I walked outside and rang around until I found a vet in the area who'd treat my cat without the six-hundred-dollar biopsy. The next vet was a tall, slim, balding redhead, with freckled, sun-damaged skin. He was softly spoken and kind and I fought the urge to stretch up on my toes to place a gentle kiss on his cheek in thanks.

~

It's hard to define the feeling of mutual sexual attraction. Is there even a word that sums up that strange physiological awareness? The one I usually reach for is 'vibe', although, coming from northern New South Wales, I'm conscious of our embarrassing hippie lexicon. So, what is it, this vibe? It's easy enough to identify your own physical attraction to another person. Hyper-alertness to their presence, focus on their physical attributes, an elevated heart rate, tingly skin, the need to make eye contact, and — if you're me — difficulty in expressing yourself clearly, a fumbling-ness, or outright clumsiness. But what is it that makes the vibe feel mutual? I've been around people who don't show any of my overt symptoms of attraction, but in whom I still detect a sense that it's there. Perhaps I'm subconsciously picking up on subtle biological cues — dilated pupils or the faintest of flushes. I often perceive their state as a type of stillness. While I am spilling over, the other person is calm, but somehow receptive to all my trembly sensuality. It's as though I have their attention and they are making room for me. But how (without asking) could I ever confirm such an indecipherable thing?

~

I may well be the least qualified person to write about desire. My primary response to the quandaries of sexual interaction has been to choose celibacy, building and sustaining all manner of other relationships — with my mother, my children, my friends, the pets, my homeplace — but more or less disengaging from sexual or romantic intimacy, until — propelled by an overwhelming physical pull — once a decade or so, I have another (disastrous) go. But maybe I'll always be drawn to writing about the thing I least understand — a mystery to solve, a puzzle to complete — all the while knowing that there will be missing pieces, that I might never be any the wiser. It's terrifying to acknowledge how little we evolve or grow in a lifetime; how persistent our patterns can be, how unchanging. A life seems so vast (especially in the beginning), but, really, it's all just the briefest flash. Are our expectations of ourselves as ever-evolving beings just too high?

~

There's no male gaze in the forest. Truth be told, there's hardly any gaze at all. The trees are without eyes. I brush against their leaves as I walk, reaching out to caress their trunks. They are solid, not skittish, and they seem receptive to my touch. In the creek that surrounds us, I swim naked. There is no one to see. In my forest home, my awareness of self is almost wholly sensory: the feeling of ground underfoot, the gentle flow of the creek, the jostle of the dog against my legs, the velvet rub of the cat running its body along my arm. The pets observe me closely, but they don't make judgements about my desirability, as far as I can tell. At home, I experience my body as acceptable. I don't focus on any kind of reflected view. Out in the world, especially in cities, I am often overcome by a sense of my wrongness. I have no resilience against the messaging of advertising. The billboards scream, 'you will never be enough!' A few days away from home and I am convinced I need to cut calories and invest in false eyelashes and any number of beauty-orientated things. *You have been so deluded!* my psyche shouts. *There is nothing acceptable about you!* I always come home full of plans about how I might meet this outside-world standard, but in the gentle light of the forest, the anxiety falls away and I am back to defining myself through touch.

~

The rooms of our house are all separate rectangular modules built along a central walkway, forest growing between them. Most of the walls are sliding glass doors. There is little distinction between inside and out. My mother likes to wander in the forest garden, picking up fallen palm fronds and inspecting the seedlings. She planted the trees with my father, but now the forest self-seeds, growing wild. All our pets accompany my mother on these garden jaunts, even William the cat. The pup, anxious for jobs, tugs giant fronds to the edge so my mother can throw them over the banks to decompose. Everything in the family is the family, I think, watching her from the house. My mother and her animal tribe.

~

Our mother–daughter relationship has never ruptured. Perhaps I've never individuated the way a person is supposed to? My mother has always been the most reliable presence in my life, even when I've had a boyfriend or long-term partner. While dedicated to me, she also follows her own path, and she seems to strike that balance effortlessly.

—

I'm a terrible flirt, and I don't mean that in a cheeky, ironic sense, I'm just plain terrible. But it wasn't always this way. When I first started high school, I happily exchanged flirty banter with the boys in my classes. It was part of our everyday language. A way of feeling things out, testing the waters. As far as I could tell, there was nothing contractual about it. If I involved myself in a playful, teasing conversation with a boy, I didn't owe him anything later. Sometimes it might lead to a romantic interaction, but mostly not.

At fourteen I moved schools and my worldview took a battering. There was a boy in my maths class who I liked a lot. He was smart and nice and funny and I was friendly with him, friendly in the same way I would have been with anyone I felt was smart and nice and funny. A few weeks into my new school life, he approached me at lunchtime.

'Don't talk to me again,' he said.

'What?' I stuttered.

'Just don't talk to me, okay?'

His rage was palpable, his face strained.

'Okay,' I replied softly. I stood there, staring at him, wondering what I'd done.

'You can't talk to me. Not if you don't mean it.'

'Mean what?' I'd thought we were friends.

'Just don't talk to me again.' He was clenching his fist in frustration.

I nodded, subdued, and he turned and strode away. Although we remained in the same maths class for the rest of our school years, we never spoke again.

Whatever flirting we'd done clearly had a degree of seriousness for him that it didn't have for me. After that I was careful. Watchful, tentative. I no longer approached the boys in my classes with the same openness or ease. Words have power, I thought, flirting seemed like nothing, but it wasn't.

~

My first high school was a fortress of brutalist architecture — multiple levels of concrete with dark stairwells at each corner. Between every class, six times a day, we had to find our way to a new classroom. I was twelve and often got lost in the sameness. Packs of older boys roamed freely, rounding us up in the stairwells and shoving their hands up our skirts. Finding my next class was like running the gauntlet.

~

Even with my no-flirting policy, the boys at the new school were easily aggrieved. 'Slut,' they'd hiss as I passed. 'Pricktease.' Just by existing, I somehow embodied both these things at once. On guard, I crept around, hiding behind my hair.

An older boy on my bus took a liking to me. He was burly and sad and I found him frightening. He radiated pain. At school, I maintained a wide berth, but I couldn't avoid the bus.

One day, a few older boys got word that my friends and I were hanging out at a girlfriend's house, unsupervised. They dropped over unannounced. Three of us and three of them. The boy from the bus was one of them. The air seemed to zing with possibilities. No parents, six teenagers. Anything could happen. In the kitchen, I willed my friends not to leave me alone with him, but after a while they did.

'I don't feel that way about you,' I said, when he tried to touch me.

'If you don't, I'm going to kill myself.' He opened a drawer and pulled out a large, serrated knife. 'I'll slit my wrists, right here.'

He started sawing at the skin on his wrist. A scream built inside me. He was beginning to draw blood. All protest was wedged in my throat. I was gasping for air. At that moment, the others came back to the kitchen. I ran to the bathroom and locked myself in.

Undoubtedly, the boy with the knife was troubled, but I've never been able to erase the way he looked at me while he sliced into his own skin: eyes hungry and brimming with accusation. As though I owed him a debt, and he would punish us both because I would not repay it. After that, I stopped flirting altogether.

Unrequited desire was a dangerous thing. But those words were still hurled at me in the halls of my school: slag, pricktease, hot, snob, too good for us, are ya?

~

A little while back, I made an appointment to see an energy healer on a whim. The type of practitioner who claimed to commune with your ancestors, but also healed you through working with your energy, whatever that was. I was sceptical, of course. The healer worked from a hotel room in the city I was visiting. After I contacted him, my appointment was organised via text by an intermediary called 'Terri'. It was a dodgy setup: I was to meet him downstairs in the lobby and he would take me up to his room. He arrived, bigger than I expected, but with something of the ageing farm boy about him. Shy, but physically strong, like he could roll up bales of hay. And, yes, as I followed him along those winding hotel hallways I did think — what if he tries to touch me? Am I colluding in my own abuse? Am I, in fact, paying for it?

Once in the room, I told him nothing at all about me, stated no reason for my visit. I didn't want to taint his 'reading' with any extraneous information, and he did not ask me to.

He had a massage table set up, and he requested I climb on and lie face-up. He explained that he might need to rest his hands on me briefly, but I was to let him know at any stage if I felt uncomfortable.

I nodded.

He stood alongside my body and placed a hand on each of my shins. After a few minutes of silence, he took his hands away.

He began to talk about my great-great-grandparents and the messages they had for me.

'Okay, we're hearing from Albert? You got an Albert?' he asked.

I shrugged. 'Maybe.' I was neutral. 'I'm sorry, I just don't know.'

I wasn't all that interested in random words of wisdom from unknown ancestors, whose existence could be neither confirmed nor denied. As I stifled a yawn, he put his hand on my upper thigh and said, 'I'm just going to tune in to your body.'

The touch did not feel inappropriate, but the weirdness of such touch in a hotel room, and the fact that I'd put myself there by choice, was disquieting. After a few more minutes of 'tuning in', he looked at me, as though trying to weigh up how much to say.

'I think you've been sexually assaulted while unconscious,' he said. 'To do with alcohol. When you were a young teen.'

This shocked me, so out of nowhere, but like the unknown ancestors it was the kind of narrative that couldn't be verified.

'I'm sorry,' the man said. 'I know it must be hard to hear.'

'What makes you say that?' I asked, heartbeat banging in my chest. 'About being assaulted?'

'The kinds of wounds your body holds. The energy. That's what it's saying to me.'

I was struggling to know how to respond. His fingers were still warm on my thigh.

'Is it possible?' he asked. 'Do you think?'

The truth was, I'd spent several years as a young teen binge-drinking to unconsciousness. At the time, I'd felt protected by friends — and the presence of my high-school boyfriend — but there were gaps in their surveillance, and they were always drunk too.

'It's possible,' I conceded. I couldn't rule it out.

But that didn't mean it happened. I may have grown up in a hippie stronghold, but was wise enough to know that being told something by an energy healer I'd happened across did not make it fact. The man in the hotel room said a lot of things that day, with his hand on my thigh, a lot of them to do with unwanted incursions on my body. I thought, how can he know so much about me? And then I thought, he could say this shit to any woman and it would probably be true.

~

My older son, Milla, liked to hang out in a pack, so when he was home there were never fewer than four extras, sometimes many more. We lived thirty minutes from the nearest town, and these teenage boys often came to our place to recover from whatever wild business they'd been up to in the world outside. They were a motley bunch, rowdy and rough around the edges, but sweet-seeming too. Impeccably polite. They were — I'm guessing — used to being unwelcome house guests, and were careful not to overstep boundaries. They never ate anything without asking. They never showered or spent time in the shared areas of the house. Though they all towered over me and I could hear their booming voices from my son's garage bedroom, when they spoke to me it was always softly. Heads slightly bowed, looking at me through fringes, deferential. But as these boys approached adulthood, I sensed a shift in the way they responded to me. Not all of them, but a few. It was as though, as they became men, they suddenly noticed I was a woman. It happened fast: they bulked up, lost their lankiness, grew beards, however slight, and I perceived a stillness when I walked into my son's room, an attention to my physical presence, that wasn't there before. But it went both ways. All of a sudden, they seemed fully grown men and I was more conscious of their bodies too. This mutual physical awareness hovered around us, unremarkable, natural even. We all ignored it, but that doesn't mean it wasn't there.

~

When my sons were younger, still pre-teens, we'd drive to a local swimming hole to jump off a rope that hung from an ancient camphor. It was a secret haunt, hidden behind the old church, past two sets of fences, one barbed and one not. We shimmied through the fences, on the lookout for snakes in the overgrown grass. In summer it was a spot favoured by teens, boys in particular, and I would only agree to stay there if it was deserted. I didn't want to have to negotiate a gang of teenage boys, to mother under their gaze, trying to rein in my young sons while the rest of them were wild and reckless and free. But occasionally, when my sons and I were already there, a bunch of boys would show up. After a while I got used to them. They turned out to be gentle enough, and let my sons have their go on the rope. In those days I inhabited a liminal space. I was a young mother, years older than the boys there, but years younger than their own mothers. After a time, they seemed to forget I was present, or forget I was an adult. I stayed quiet, listening to their conversations, seeking a window into my children's future. Adolescence, right there on our horizon. When it was just me and my sons, I often swung off the rope and into the water. I'd been doing such things since childhood, and even surrounded by teenage boys, I would sometimes clamber over for a turn. When I made my way to the swinging rope, that stillness would permeate the air. These boys watched me, surreptitiously, but with great attention. At the edge of the creek bank, I stood straight, chin up, gazing out over the water. The boys fell quiet around me, taking me in. What was it, in that moment, that made me sense the pull of their sexual interest? I experienced it as a quality of the air. A faint but perceptible fizzle.

~

Luca, two years younger than Milla, preferred not to hang out in a pack. Arriving home from high school, my younger son would drift into his bedroom to play endless Xbox games of FIFA. We had terrible internet, so he played the soccer game solo. He seemed to view home as a refuge from the world of other people, although in company he was chatty and easygoing. Luca played soccer in the real world too. From the sidelines, I once observed him spy a ladybug and move it to safety during his soccer coach's last-game pep-talk. Part of the group, but not part of it. Subtly going his own way. It didn't matter how many times I watched Luca play soccer, I couldn't learn the rules of the game. Humans running after a ball like swarming bees. The same went for Xbox FIFA. Some evenings I lay on Luca's bed with him and watched the fantasy game, the canopy of the forest rustling above us. Nestling close to my younger son was a salve to my nervous system. Two quiet bodies, in proximity, in the same room.

~

The father of my children had a giant smile that he flashed indiscriminately. He shared his happiness around as if it would never run out. We first met when I was fourteen, he fifteen, and from the outset he loved me with a steadfastness that was hard to comprehend. Back then, my smiling boyfriend and I once climbed into a pair of tracksuits pants to see if we could fit. We were staying the night in the little house, a cabin my father had built for my mother when I was a child. The little house had a pitched roof and two queen-sized beds that dropped from the ceiling. The frames of the beds were sturdy and immovable, but hanging in space. Floating side by side, the beds functioned like a loft or mezzanine, but with none of the solidity. In between them was a small fixed platform reached via a ladder. The beds were close enough to the ceiling that, once in them, you couldn't stand, but there was room to sit or crouch. Above one of them was a clear perspex skylight, so you could lie on your back and gaze at the stars.

Up in those bunks, in the darkness of night, my boyfriend and I had fused inside the tracksuit pants, and found, with rising panic, that we couldn't get out. There was only a sliver of moon, so we couldn't see the edges of the beds. We were terrified that we might just topple over the sides and crash below, unable to break our fall because we were trapped together in the tracksuit pants. We rolled gently in the blackness, trying various methods to shimmy out, the danger of the unseen edges at the forefront of our minds. It's an absurd image, but somehow prescient. We had jumped in together impulsively, two kids, only to find we didn't quite know where we were in space. It was slow going, but eventually, in the dawning light, we inched ourselves out.

~

In that first relationship, I was expected to put out. It was my job as a girlfriend, and for the first few years I put out whenever it was required. It was as though my boyfriend's erection, already existing, demanded something of me, and it was a long time before I was independent enough to reject this claim. At the time, I seemed to react with a Pavlovian-type response, almost subconscious. I was very young and I wanted to be the kind of girlfriend who liked sex and was always ready to have it. But that version of me wore thin. Maybe I learned to listen better to my body. Maybe I stopped being so eager to please. It began to irk me that, when initiating sex, my boyfriend didn't seem interested in how enthusiastic I was, that he saw my body as something he was entitled to. How can desire flourish under those conditions? Sex became something to avoid. And I was so often under siege, pressed to participate in sex I did not desire, that any sexual urges I may have had dispersed quickly. There was no room for them to grow.

~

When Milla was born I'd just turned twenty, my smiling boyfriend twenty-one. To say we were unprepared is perhaps putting things lightly. On arrival at the hospital, the stark lights and the gum-cracking drawl of the midwife sent me into a panic. My boyfriend, already stunned, watched on as I cried into the puddle of liquid that was my waters breaking.

'It's so messy,' I sobbed, as a nurse mopped up the warm water still gushing from inside me.

'Honey, this is just the beginning,' the midwife said, still chewing her gum.

Blinded by shock and pain and strapped up to machines, I couldn't move. Reality shuffled out of the room.

Induced. A kind of torture.

I pleaded with my boyfriend to help me.

'What can I do?' he asked, wide-eyed and jittery.

'I don't know. Just do it!'

He tried to rub my arm, and I threw off his hand, 'Don't touch me. Not that.'

My boyfriend began to pace around the birthing suite.

'You may as well have a rest,' the midwife said to him. 'It'll be a long night.'

He lay down on a couch against the wall, and in moments he was dozing. My body was awash with wrenching pain while my boyfriend slept peacefully on the couch. Minutes becoming hours. Labour. Relentless. The gum-cracker's shift ended. She left and a new midwife arrived. Nurses and doctors came and went from the room, all strangers. When the time came to push, they woke my boyfriend and I struggled and strained, while he watched apprehensively. Two hours passed with no sense of progress. From my place on the bed, surveyed from above, there seemed no end in sight. I began to have doubts. Who were these people? How could I trust them? Even my boyfriend, who'd slept so easily, seemed suspect.

'You're getting close,' the new midwife said finally, 'keep trying.'

I kept pushing, but I didn't believe her.

'I see it, Jess,' she told me. The top of my baby's head. 'One more push' she added, 'and the head will be out.'

I glanced at my boyfriend, searching for truth, and he nodded.

My strapping baby arrived, blue and floppy, the cord wrapped around his neck, not once but twice. He'd been stuck in the birth canal, tethered by the shortened cord. As they rushed him from the room, I willed them to bring him back to me. After a few minutes they returned, Milla pink and breathing. The midwife put him to my breast and he suckled forcefully. I watched his little mouth working, then leaned to the side and retched, overcome by nausea.

After the birth, all the buoyancy of pregnancy was gone. My skin was stretched and loose, the muscles of my core so weak I could barely sit up, the swelling between my legs so severe I could only hobble to the bathroom, clutching at the walls. The body-self I'd known was gone. A thundering started up inside my head, all my terror rising. Who was this tiny creature lying beside me? What had I done?

~

Two years later, when Luca arrived, the labour was fast, almost painless. He was suddenly in the world, everyone in the hospital room smiling with surprise.

'Good job, Jess! That was great!'

After the revolving door of strangers that had accompanied Milla's birth, I'd paid to see an obstetrician during my second pregnancy, not understanding that it was unlikely he would be scheduled on for my birth. The local hospital's birthing unit was run on a roster, a mix of my obstetrician and the GPs in town who were qualified to deliver babies. The doctor rostered on had barely made it to the hospital in time.

I peered at my second son, large and screaming on my belly. My boyfriend and a midwife took him outside to weigh and measure him. Another midwife and the doctor stayed to finish the birthing. The afterbirth.

Tugging lightly on the umbilical cord, they chatted and laughed while they waited for the placenta to detach. I thought of my new son crying in the next room, the way his chin was round and dimpled. I wondered if he looked a bit like my dead father.

Out of nowhere, I heard a distant pop.

'Fuck, it's snapped off. Fuck. Fuck! Fuck!' the doctor stammered. 'I'm sorry, I'm so sorry.'

The midwife looked across at him in fright. They braced themselves against me, holding me pinned.

'What?' I shouted, struggling against them. 'What's wrong?'

They held me down and the doctor began to push his gloved hand right up inside me. I cried out, trying to wrestle myself from their hold. He yanked out the placenta and the whole queen-sized bed was soaked with blood.

'Why?' I whispered, shaking, hoarse. Blood squelched beneath my shoulders as I tried to sit up.

My boyfriend stepped back into the room with Luca in a trolley. He took in the bloodied bed and turned pale. I motioned him over.

Pulling him close, I whispered in terror, 'They hurt me. Don't let them near me again.'

I peeked behind my boyfriend, trying to keep tabs on the doctor's movements. Before the cord snapped, he'd seemed innocuous, a nondescript middle-aged man, but afterwards he seemed dangerous, unpredictable, cruel. I was watching for any sudden movements.

My boyfriend said nothing, straightening up, but his hand shook as he smoothed a loose curl back behind my ear.

'The cord snapped off and slipped back inside her,' the doctor explained to my boyfriend. 'It's like cutting off your arm, the blood just pumps out.'

'Shit, that's a lot of blood,' my boyfriend muttered.

'We'll take all this stuff," the doctor motioned to the bedsheets, "and get it weighed, so we know how much blood she's lost. That's how we calculate it. Will you help us move her? Can we cut off her T-shirt?'

'No, don't cut her shirt.' My boyfriend was stern. 'She loves that shirt, it's special to her. It was her Dad's.'

Carefully, they took my blood-soaked shirt off and wound it through the intravenous drips the nurse had attached on my arms. Blood on one side, antibiotics on the other.

On the freshly made bed my boyfriend curled up at my side.

'You should call the rest of her family,' the doctor pronounced gently. 'They need to be here, in case.'

'In case what?' My boyfriend sat up.

'We'll do everything we can, but … she's got to go into surgery soon. She's lost a lot of blood … it's just … hard to predict.'

The doctor's words seemed muffled.

My boyfriend lay back down, his face close to mine. 'Do you want me to get your mum?' He was crying, silent dripping tears.

'Do you want to see her before you go in?'

'No, it's fine,' I whispered, dry-mouthed and dazed. 'She's looking after Milla. I'll see her soon.'

The doctor leaned down to speak to me. 'We're going to try to fix you up in surgery.' He smelled of stale cigarettes and coffee. 'The placenta didn't come out properly.'

'Why?' I whispered. His proximity, so close to my face, was terrifying.

'It came out in pieces. We have to get it all out, or you'll keep bleeding. We're just waiting for some blood to go in before we start.'

'Will it be like before?' I asked. The image of them holding me down was already flashing on repeat inside my mind.

'Oh no, Jess, you'll be under. It was an emergency before,' the doctor reached a hand out and I flinched to evade his touch.

'I've never had to do that before,' he said. 'I was very scared.'

'It hurt, it hurt a lot.'

'I'm so sorry, Jess. I'm so so sorry.'

My new baby was asleep in a plastic tray in the corner of the room. In his first minutes he had screamed wildly, his eyes squeezed shut, and then he'd lapsed into an impenetrable sleep. My boyfriend and I lay still on the bed, facing each other, nose to nose, knee to knee, but not quite touching. Waiting for the blood to flow in.

—

For the first day after Luca's birth, I was so weakened by the blood loss, I couldn't sit or stand.

'You lost half your blood volume,' the nurse on duty explained. 'First lot post-birth, second lot in surgery. You are lucky to be alive.'

The nurse bathed my body lovingly with a washer, one section at a time, holding my gaze as if willing me to stay conscious. I stared at her as though from a great distance. My new baby kept sleeping, only snuffling and squirming for an occasional feed. The nurse lifted him across from his plastic tray and helped me attach him to my breast. He still hadn't opened his eyes, as though he wasn't yet ready to see.

How was my body to make sense of the degree of violence that had accompanied Luca's birth? To save my life a doctor pushed his whole hand up inside my bruised, swollen, post-birth vagina and tore an adherent placenta from the wall of my womb. In those moments, my embattled body-self believed him to be assaulting me, with the midwife's frantic, frightened assistance. Afterwards I lay in a pool of my own blood so vast it covered a queen-sized bed. Where does a body store that information? That memory?

~

Four years after Luca's birth, I separated from the father of my children. The freedom from sexual obligation made me positively ecstatic. I did not miss sex. I did not miss the constant struggle for bodily autonomy. The feeling of never having to put out again left me woozy with gratitude. My happiness was complete. Desireless. No sex on the horizon. But in time, slowly but surely, my desire for others came creeping back in.

~

Getting to know someone new can be a complicated affair. Sometimes it's hard to judge what to reveal about yourself and what might best be left to a later date. When do we divulge the basic facts of our lives? I favour getting it out of the way early. Omission of truth has always felt like lying, and if people don't know what I've been through, I fear the relationship is built on a kind of false floor, which could, at any moment, cave in.

Usually, it comes up naturally enough.

'So, how many siblings do you have?'

I always pause, because now I have two — a younger brother and an older sister — but I used to have three. How this came about is the crux of my story. For me, this innocuous question holds a different kind of weight.

When I was twelve, my eighteen-year-old half-sister, Zoe, killed herself. I could mention this, or I could hold off. If I disclose, the conversation might slam to a halt. I'm always afraid my revelation will cause a rupture, an end. But sometimes I risk it and say, 'Three. I had three.'

My sister has been dead now longer than she was alive, but growing up with Zoe coloured my whole childhood. My family was devastated by her loss — her suicide like a hand grenade detonating right in the heart of us. No one was unscathed. I often try to imagine the adult my sister would have become if she'd chosen life over death all those years ago. Sometimes I catch a glimpse of a stranger and see a fleeting resemblance. She'd have been like that, I think. And what I most long to say to the sibling question is, 'Three. I have three.'

But if by chance that question doesn't arise, there's always the seemingly safe territory of, 'So, where's your dad these days?'

Heartbroken after my sister's suicide, my father became ill. Crippling depressions interspersed with effervescent but terrifying highs, a late onset, grief-induced bipolar disorder. In and out of psychiatric hospitals, he finally took his own life six years later. One suicide lighting the fuse of another, a sort of explosive domino effect.

In my head, I call them 'the dark years', when everything I knew and took for granted crumbled. You can see why I might be nervous about false floors after my whole family had plunged into an unimaginable black hole. My father was fifty-four when he died. The older I get, the younger that seems.

~

Before he died, my father, a psychiatrist, gave me a self-help book, *Silent Grief: Living in the Wake of Suicide*. The book contained a series of case studies of bereaved people, which included a bewildering array of physical reactions or symptoms — insomnia, headache, migraine, nausea, fibromyalgia, loss of libido, heart attack, stroke, the list went on and on. When my father gave me the book, my sister had been dead four years, and I read it with a rising sense of horror at all the things that might go wrong. After he killed himself two years later, complicated grief, with all its somatic trappings, became my normal.

After my father's death, I became locked in a cycle of intense migraines for years. These headaches were the primary way I experienced my body. Over time (and with much therapeutic intervention) the headaches lessened, but the tendency to become aware of my body only through pain persisted. When I got a migraine, I was called on to remember that I had a body. Mostly my response would be, 'Oh no, not you again! Do you have to come along?' I often felt my body was letting me down, that it wasn't on my side. That life would be better if I could just let my body go. This experience of disembodiment meant spontaneous surges of sexual desire always felt miraculous: my body, the casing I was rarely attuned to, except through pain or injury, suddenly became sensitised. My blood pulsed. I was shuddery, hot all over, alive. It was easy to see why sex with another person might promise a more embodied existence. It was an activity that focused on sensation. The other person might invite me back to my body, or be able to coax feeling, or to inhabit their own body in a way that somehow rubbed off.

It's true that in the forest my choices were limited. It's possible the first man I desired, post-separation from the father of my children, was the only single man I knew. That said, I can still remember the magnetic pull of his physicality. I used to stare, transfixed, at the shadowed curve of his eyelashes against his cheekbones. He may not have been everyone's cup of tea, but he was certainly mine. When I first met him, I thought him laughably confident and brash. Even though he had a shorn head, when I imagined him, it was with an Elvis-style pompadour and an Elvis-style swagger. I'd had trouble taking him seriously, but his gaze was uncommonly direct and to my complete surprise I found myself thinking about him at all hours, wondering what he looked like under his clothes. Once I identified it, my desire for this man grew at an exponential pace, until it felt like destiny, always a dangerous place to find yourself. These days, as soon as the word 'destiny' flashes inside my mind, I take it as a warning signal: things are about to get out of hand.

As soon as we organised to meet up, my body began to crumble. It was a fortnight until our date, but my nausea became so debilitating I thought it was a bona-fide stomach bug. My tongue swelled up hideously, raw and metallic-tasting, the top layer of skin peeling entirely off. I stopped sleeping, stopped eating, and counted down the days till our date, wondering if there was enough time to get better. I went to a doctor about my tongue, but she was perplexed. All the symptoms seemed to have arisen in direct response to my upcoming date, but I didn't register any feelings of anxiety or fear. Excitement was how I would have described it. So why was my body throwing impediments in my path, like a strange kind of obstacle course? I thought about postponing, to give myself some recovery time, but instead I pushed through.

We met up at a local park near the ocean, and lazed about beneath the feathery trees. There were many reasons why this man was wrong for me, but one of them was his directness. It sent my body into a spin. I was twitching as I lay down on the grass beside him.

'So, what's that about?' he asked, almost straight up, motioning at my quivering body.

I was thrown. 'I'm a little nervous,' I admitted. I didn't tell him about my tongue.

'Why don't I kiss you right now, so you can relax?'

This was theoretically a good plan, but my body did not like it. As he leaned towards me, I combat-rolled away from him in shock. In that moment, it was as though I'd split in two. On the one hand, there was my consciousness: who I assumed I was, and, on the other, there was my body: this recalcitrant, unwieldy housing for my 'self'.

'Maybe not then?' he shrugged.

After a few weeks he broke off with me. My first proper romantic rejection. I assumed that this abortive experience of desire was a one-off. Just an unfortunate mismatch between his particular style of interacting and mine. My body had done some odd things, but he was a wildman, all impulse and action. It was probably not so strange that I had been startled.

None of this turned out to be true.

~

My body, I soon discovered, though capable of the sensations and pleasures of arousal and desire, responded to the possibility of a sexual encounter as though it was a bona fide threat, even though — to my knowledge — I'd never been raped. The dictionary on my study desk defined trauma as 'a startling experience which has a lasting effect'. It wasn't the severity of the event itself but the impact of it over the long term which defined it as traumatic. I thought about all the startling experiences I'd had back-to-back in my teens and early twenties. Was it possible to pinpoint which one was causing my difficulties around sex? Or were the effects of these experiences somehow cumulative? Could I ever know?

I felt like a freak, but the truth was my body had always been very expressive. Rage would bring on nosebleeds. Fear would bring on hives. But it was the possibility of sex that sent my body into freefall — the unaccountable twitching in the proximity of my might-be lover. If my body got a whiff of a kiss in the works my tongue would swell up, obstructing speech. I'd been known to stand up and just spin around on the spot. Don't even get me started on my vagina and all the painful complications it threw my way. If these symptoms were aftereffects of passion they would have been easier to manage, but my body produced them in anticipation of physical contact, so that, to get close to someone, I had to overcome an array of bewildering ailments. In adulthood, desire had become fraught — it made me sick. The quickest remedy was to withdraw. In isolation I retained a wellness that was enduring and relatively unproblematic. Life was calm. But did I really want a sexless existence? For the most part — truly — yes! It was a small price to pay for the kind of equilibrium I craved. But every now and again I would come across a person who sparked something in me. My body, which I often struggled to feel, would come alive. It misbehaved, yes. It caused me no end of trouble. But at the same time, it coursed with *feeling*. It tingled and pricked. It flushed. It filled with involuntary, wild, often pleasurable sensations. Where did it come from — this spark — ignited by another? What was it even for?

~

With all this inexpressible feeling, I wrote a book about the wildman. A novel, told from his perspective. I was not then a writer and I didn't believe it would ever be read. The relationship between us was non-existent in the real world, but it had a life of its own in my imagination. In that lively space, I did what I wanted with him. I was not impeded by my disobedient body or his lack of reciprocal feeling. The pleasure of the writing was extreme. What kind of person writes a book to inhabit someone? The answer, it turned out, was me.

Writing fiction is an act of embodiment in the 'other'. An avenue of escape, an avatar experience. Through my characters' bodies, I saw and felt another world. During the act of writing, I was free to occupy bodies far less damaged or inhibited or unpredictable than mine. With my first novel, I stepped into the assuredness of being an unreflective, unanalytical man. I moved through the world confident about my place. I left the experience of womanhood behind. In my second novel, I inhabited the wondrous excitement of being an undamaged young woman discovering sexual pleasure. The freedom! The sensuality! The hopefulness! Writing both books gave me a visceral thrill. As the scenes progressed, my body would heat up, until I was flushed with an excitement and pleasure, akin to arousal. Embodiment in the idea of others came far more easily to me than embodiment in self.

~

Even in this age of mass-sharing, there seem to be some stubborn areas of privacy, one of which remains the peculiarity of the animal bodies we all inhabit, our strange and sometimes subconscious urges. In my case, it is the bizarre and bewildering somatic minefield I have to navigate to even attempt to see out my sexual desires. For years I have believed that my situation was unique, made so by a combination of innate sensitivity and the specific difficulties I have experienced, but lately I have begun to wonder. Tentatively, I have asked around. Am I the only one with such an uncooperative body-self? Every woman I've raised this with has been surprised by my swollen tongue, by my compulsive combat rolls. But some women friends have admitted to me that their first response — even to a welcome sexual advance — is to flinch. And that their lovers have often assumed they have been assaulted or raped, even when, to the best of their knowledge, they have not. Their body seems to hold some historical first-response of flight. Maybe I was not as alone as I believed?

~

When we take in the sexual transgressions against women throughout history, even if in the past these acts were normalised or minimised, it is hard to imagine that all of our bodies would not hold some genetic memory of sexual resistance or, at least, reticence. Trauma can leave a chemical mark on our genes. Generations of mice, bred in labs, with no exposure to cats, still know to fear their scent. Our bodies hold ancestral trauma that is passed through our DNA. How are we to navigate it? Historical rapes and molestations. The dizzying horrors enacted against colonised or enslaved or war-ravaged peoples. As well as less violent experiences. The duty of sleeping with a husband you don't desire. Sexual exchange for protection or food. The generally transactional nature of sex throughout human history. Because it was safer. Because it was expected. Because it was advantageous. Because, really, what choice did women have? In amongst all this violence and sexual transaction, it seems a miracle that female desire has been so resilient. And yes, there must have always been individual women who were able to act on their desires. Female desire *is* resilient. But I think we must concede that, for much of our history, a woman acting solely on her sexual desires probably wasn't the norm. The power (im)balance did not allow it. If women's sexual expression has been largely dictated by pragmatism, how do we acknowledge that the aftereffects — genetic memory, that inexplicable flinch — may still be held in our bodies? And how can we reclaim a more joyful and pleasureful route?

~

Luca has a susceptibility to cellulitis, bacterial infections of the tissue beneath the skin, which began the year he turned four and continued, on and off, throughout the following year. It was also the year his father left, though I did not notice the correlation at the time. When Luca was ten, he got an infection in the tissue around one eye. Half his face swelled up like a lopsided balloon and I rushed him to Emergency. He was kept in hospital on an antibiotic drip for three days. A week before Luca's cellulitis flared up, my mother's partner, Shawn, died.

~

My sons never met my father. He died two years before Milla's birth. They had flexible notions of family and believed Shawn was their grandfather. Milla was twelve at Shawn's funeral, but he wailed like a desolate toddler, his keening so loud, so deeply expressive, the intensity of it ran through us all like an electric current. We were in the same crematorium where we'd held my father's funeral and I was hanging on by a thread. In that memory-laden place, I was paralysed, sitting, for some reason, a few pews in front of my son. Milla's father, my old smiling boyfriend, tried to comfort him, but Milla's misery only intensified. My ex began to cry uncontrollably too. They howled there together, clutching each other, heads thrown back, mouths wide. Luca crept up and sat beside me, looping my arm around him and holding it in place. Together we were quiet, stunned. A few days later Luca's face began to swell.

~

After Luca was discharged from hospital, I took him to the house where my mother had lived with Shawn during his illness, and we set him up in Shawn's old sick bed. There was air-conditioning, and in the suffocating summer heat it seemed a sensible choice, but it was also the bed in which Shawn had recently died. Milla, recovered from his funeral-wailing, lay beside his younger brother on that death-bed and whispered in Luca's ear. He stayed there day and night, whispering and whispering, as though he believed that if he stopped speaking Luca might slip away. Milla told him stories, right up close to his ear, and they giggled together, their bodies jiggling with laughter. He cajoled his brother back to health, one word at a time.

~

Milla had changed schools each year for the first three years of high school, but by the third year he finally settled. I had to drive him ten kilometres to connect with a bus that took him to the new school. Luca often came along for the ride.

We'd arrive at the bus stop and Milla would clamber out, swinging his bag over his shoulder, slamming the car door hard.

'I love you,' I would call out my window.

Milla always grunted in response. An acknowledgement of sorts.

'He didn't say it back, Mum,' Luca said, one day, looking at me sideways.

'He never does,' I shrugged. 'He never has.'

As a pre-schooler, Luca had said 'I love you' approximately every twenty minutes. 'Marm!' A squawking baby magpie. 'I love you!' He still said 'I love you' at every goodbye, even when he climbed the school bus steps in the midst of his peers. It surprised me that he had never noticed his brother did not.

'He always just grunts,' I said, shrugging. 'Exactly like he did just then.'

Luca looked down at his lap. 'Mum, that's awkward.'

Milla was nearly a man, and he decided that a man needed a dog. Unannounced, he brought home the puppy. I took the puppy to the vet for his vaccinations and was struck, all over again, by the young vet's beauty. I had forgotten about him, but the jolt of my response to his physicality was, once again, rousing.

'Teenagers are the worst at raising puppies,' he told me in a tone of authority. 'They have such poor boundaries and they pass that on. Your son will need to bring him to puppy school, but you should also bring your son in for a chat with me.'

Great! I thought. A man willing to talk with my son. About responsibility and puppies! About being a man.

The vet was so confident, I felt confident too.

The following week I brought Milla in for his chat. We opened the door and the vet looked up at my son in surprise.

'You said I should bring him in for a chat,' I said, trying to prompt him.

The vet was gawking.

'About having a puppy?'

Had he imagined some kind of pimply, scrawny kid, easy to intimidate? My son was over six foot, and large. Milla's face was open and friendly, but his size was breathtaking, especially next to me. Milla sat down on one of the chairs, relaxed. *Give it to me*, his grin seemed to say.

'Well, ah …' the vet stuttered.

All the vet's confidence seemed to drain from him in front

of the specimen of manhood that was my boy. Even his beauty seemed to fade.

'It's just …'

My son nodded encouragingly, but I was getting impatient.

'You were going to talk to him about having a puppy?'

How I wished for one man in my son's life to be able to talk properly with him.

The vet continued to flounder, obviously incapacitated by the size of my son.

Goddammit, I thought. I will do this too, this talk about responsibility, like I have done everything else.

I'd desired him, this cocky young vet, I'd felt the wildness in my body flair, but not all desire was meaningful. The trick was knowing which feelings mattered.

~

Still without his licence, Milla claimed his freedom from the forest by hitchhiking endlessly between his friends' houses. When he'd brought the pup home, he'd envisaged that it would go every-where with him, his faithful friend, part of his independence.

'Don't take him,' I begged. 'It's not fair for him to be dragged across the countryside.'

I didn't know I needed a puppy, but it seemed that I did.

'He needs structure!' I declared. 'Leave him here with me.'

My son had chosen the scrappiest pup imaginable, a Koolie cross. We had never had a working dog in the forest before. The puppy watched our every move with crazy Mel Gibson eyes, waiting to be told what was next. He was obsessional about sticks. Obsessional about balls. But mostly he was obsessional about us, like a desperate, stalking lover.

My son relinquished ownership of the pup easily enough. He'd found the puppy a hindrance to free and easy movement. Tully needed to sleep and snack and play. He needed training. The pup became mine, mine and my mother's. Never had I felt so attended to, my every move scrutinised, my whereabouts tracked. If you google Koolies, one of the first traits listed is 'intense eye contact'. Not a moment passed when this new pup wasn't alert to my face, seeking my gaze. My sons were taking flight, but Tully was always right there, his crazy gaze seeming to promise: I will never leave you.

⁓

When Milla brought Tully home we already had a dog and a cat. Jet, the dog, was black (obviously) and plump. She had huge brown eyes, and long, velvety beagle ears, and she liked to lean her solid frame against my legs and look backwards at me, through her eyelashes. William, our tabby cat, was particularly beautiful: high cheekbones and an aloof, intelligent air. William was my mother's favourite. She appreciated his aesthetic appeal, but mostly his stand-offish demeanour. All the animals saw my mother as the leader — the matriarch — which seemed odd, as I often fed and walked them. They looked to her when any important decisions were made — when to eat, when to walk, when to play — bypassing me completely.

~

Living with my mother and the children in the forest, my contact with the world beyond diminished. My children's father had been sociable, a link to that other world. Once he left, I slipped out of any sense of belonging there. I still drove thirty minutes to the nearest town once a week for grocery shopping, but other than that, I went for long stretches without any interaction with other adults, apart from my mother. The rate at which it was possible to lose social skills was alarming, and, once lost, those skills were hard to regain. What would I say to another adult? What might be considered normal? When I had my first novel published, I was plunged into a world that was utterly foreign to me. I had to learn on the job. I was watchful and afraid, but I was also joyous. Festivals! Adults! Writers! So many strange and curious people. After the isolation of the forest, it felt like a carnival.

~

When the home phone rang and it was Lou, I always breathed a sigh of relief. Phone calls were fraught for me, but Lou's were the exception. Phobias are often irrational, the fear outweighing the threat, but my problems with the phone were specific to what I'd experienced. Before my father took his life, he called me. He was depressed, and I was impatient. I didn't grasp the subtext of his phone call. I didn't know that it was the last time I would hear his voice. I didn't understand that he was trying to say goodbye. On top of this, I received the news of my father's suicide over the phone. I was in Japan, visiting my oldest sister, and though we received the call together, the shock of it had been impossible to shake. In the years that followed, my understandable fear of receiving unexpected-late-night-phone-calls bled into a fear of receiving any phone calls, and worst of all (bizarrely), of making calls. What if there was a subtext I wasn't hearing? The pressure to decode potentially catastrophic subliminal messages through the phone-line was overwhelming. I couldn't breathe. By the time I reached my thirties, I'd developed a full-blown phone phobia.

There were, however, some people I called: my sister, who still lived in Japan, my brother, my children's father, and two or three of my closest female friends. I'd met Lou in high school, but now she lived two hours away, so, apart from when she came home to visit her parents at the family farm, most of our relationship was conducted through the phone. She was an attuned communicator, and if she had any bad news to impart, she would always say, 'Everyone's okay,' (a pause to allow my panic to subside) 'but —' and then relay the mildly upsetting information. I loved this about her, the way she effortlessly worked around my trauma idiosyncrasies. The way she didn't even seem to notice that she had.

~

When I first met Lou, we were both fourteen, but not all her adult teeth had come through. The remnants of childhood still hung about her, and I was drawn to the innocence of her gap-toothed smile. She was dreamy and whimsical, with large, owlish glasses, and she wore sprigs of jasmine in her hair. At that age, family tragedy had already taken its toll on me, but there was a freshness to Lou, a lightness. I remember thinking — she's just like me, only better. Funnier, kinder, more honest, undamaged. Lou said aloud all the secret things I kept to myself, strange thoughts or feelings I worried might set me apart. She didn't seem to have a private self, she didn't seem to need one. I loved her transparency, the freedom it afforded her, the freedom it afforded me in her company. Finding her then — during those dark years — was like surfacing from the depths of a murky pond into the soft daylight. A coiled part of me unfurled in the sun.

The importance of female friendship is often lost in our culture's rush to celebrate love and romance. The endgame of fulfilment is seen to rest squarely with marriage, or at least a committed love partnership or 'pair-bonding'. But the relationships that have most sustained me have been those that fell outside the realms of traditional notions of love. Lou once gave me a nest that she'd made from twine, with a porcelain bird sitting in it. 'It's a little bit weird, I don't know what I was thinking,' she said shyly. But it was perfect. We weren't pair-bonding, but we had built a nest, a safe place where we could hear each other's most peculiar thoughts, try to nurture one another's dreams, and where we could speak hard truths if they were necessary. Lou's voice on the end of the line brought an echo of the past, the thrill of trust and intimacy, the promise of endurance.

'Do you have time?' Lou would say.

And I'd say, 'Yeah.'

~

A little while back, I met a man twenty years my senior. I encountered him away from the forest, where everything already felt strange. I saw him catch sight of me from across the hotel lobby and time seemed to slow. I stood still, utterly surprised. Invisible concentric rings seemed to spread from him towards me through the air. It was as if I suddenly had another sensory tool at my disposal, as if I could feel the particles in the air shifting in new patterns. I'd never experienced this sensation before, and I wasn't sure what to make of it. Maybe everyone felt the circles from time to time and no one ever mentioned them? He was wearing a suit. Outside of funerals, I didn't come across suits in my ordinary life. There may have even been cufflinks. Perhaps he is remarkable? I thought. Perhaps I am insane?

The man looked as startled as I was, but he walked over and, tentatively, said hello. We chatted easily enough. He asked me to head out for a drink and I agreed. We sat on barstools in a nearby pub and I swung my legs like a child. Sit up straight, I told myself. Concentrate. But I was thinking about those circles and what they might mean.

I did what I often do when I'm nervous — gave too much of myself away.

'I've never ordered a drink at a bar,' I admitted.

He seemed to find this striking.

I didn't say, since having children, I've rarely entered a pub. I didn't say, I barely ever leave the forest. I didn't say, when I first saw you, there were strange circles in the air. Despite my nerves, I kept all that to myself.

I'd spent some time deflecting the advances of men my father's age. My father's friends, to be exact. Ever since my father died, one or two of his mates occasionally had a punt. Nothing I couldn't, politely enough, refuse. But the rage I'd felt afterwards was hard to contain. You've known me since I was a child, I wanted to shout. Would you do that if my father was here? But in that pub in a faraway place, I sat with a man, not as old as my father would have been, but older than he was when he died. The man didn't make any move to touch me. But those circles were definitely there.

When I got home to the forest, I started to notice older men on the streets of my hometown. He's alright, I'd think. I could try him out. Apart from those particular friends of my father, whom I half-despised, older men had been invisible to me. Now they were everywhere. But none of these men had rings radiating from them. The man sent me an email, inviting me for a drink if I was ever in his city. Perhaps he'd felt something too?

~

If being skin-hungry wasn't about orgasm, but about a longing for touch, I wondered if massage might help. I was skin-hungry, but I found it difficult to decipher my body's idiosyncratic messaging. I was looking for specialist help. I googled and found a local masseuse who specialised in trauma massage. I was not sure how trauma massage was different from everyday massage but I was willing to find out. In the past, I hadn't enjoyed being massaged by strangers. No matter the quality of their touch, I seemed to come out of the massage less calm than when I went in. It took me a long time to understand that my body didn't feel safe. I was supressing the urge to flee while lying face-down on the massage table, but my body was on such high alert that any therapeutic benefits of the touch were lost. I was curious about a type of massage that might acknowledge the strange quirks of my unruly body. And curious to see if that skin-hungry feeling might be alleviated by a therapeutic rather than desirous touch.

During my first session with the trauma masseuse, she told me my skin felt like it had a strange casing around it, like it was covered in playdough. 'There's no energy at the surface,' she said. Because of my intermittent issues with numbness, and my history of not enjoying massage, our future sessions would aim to help me enjoy a stranger's touch. Sometimes that meant not focusing on the parts of the body that were most painful or most numb, but instead on the areas where I felt more pleasurable sensation — I thought that might be my legs and feet. From then on, she prompted me, in a gentle voice, to stay present with her touch. This was more difficult than I would have imagined. Almost as soon as I lay face-down on the table, my thoughts began to fly off, like caged swallows suddenly set free. She prompted me often, and again and again I tried to focus on the feeling of her fingers on my skin. She was a delicate woman, not hardy-looking as I had imagined most masseuses might be. Sensitivity was written all over her face. While she massaged me, I stared at her feet through the hole in the table, at her toes neatly painted with varnish.

By the end of my third session I said, triumphantly, 'I almost enjoyed that!'

And she smiled her delicate smile.

~

I thought a lot about the older man I'd met, as though the idea of him had been planted under my skin. Like a weedy garden, my imagination was hard for me to contain. I was sprouting images, I was sprouting scenes. The more I thought about him — the more out of control my thinking — the more afraid I became. Why was my brain fixating on a virtual stranger? We emailed regularly, missives from our lives, but his writing style was so formal, so old-fashioned, that it was hard for me to figure out his intent. I presumed he was interested in me because he was contacting me, not because of anything specific he said. The uncertain nature of our interaction made me deeply anxious. He always replied to my emails promptly, often straightaway, whereas I might wait a week to reply to him, because it would take that long for me to calm down. My brother, two years younger than me, lived in this man's city. It wasn't inconceivable that I'd visit. I wanted to fly there to determine if there was anything between us, to nip in the bud any erroneous expectations. But the more we emailed and the more I thought about visiting, the more my body protested. Illness upon illness, each one more strange and bewildering. Body! I wanted to say. Help me! Get out of my way!

~

Both my father and my mother's-partner-after-my-father died before they reached sixty. Neither my uncle, my mother's younger brother, or my father's best friend, an uncle-like figure, had reached sixty either. As my interest in the older man grew, my awareness of all these premature male deaths swam sharply into focus. Sixty seemed a magic number that the men I'd loved didn't live past. I didn't know the exact age of the older man, but I presumed he was nearing sixty. I'd only met him once, but his health now preoccupied me. He could die any day! He was practically teetering on the edge of death! Why was I entertaining thoughts of becoming involved with a man so close to the age it was hard to survive past? Any attachment to him would surely end in colossal grief. This preoccupation with his death seemed both highly irrational and completely pragmatic. Someone twenty years older than me did have a higher likelihood of dying, but that didn't mean they'd die anytime soon. Then again, to become involved with someone twenty years your senior was to choose, more than likely, a precipitous goodbye. The more I puzzled through this looped thinking, the more tightness I experienced around my heart, as if a steel hand was squeezing it.

~

My trauma masseuse talked of trying to make the 'container of our selves' bigger. Of having 'more room'. Of sitting with whatever bodily sensation was present. Of trying to inhabit a non-judgemental space. She talked of sensations, even painful ones, being neither good or bad. She talked of being curious. She tried to encourage me to detach from 'the narrative' of my pain. Was it even possible to experience sensations without attaching a story, or memory, or meaning? I was perplexed by her suggestions. I am a writer, I wanted to say. Isn't the narrative everything?

Being simply curious about sensation was highly discomforting. The trauma masseuse asked me to describe my sensations using non-judgemental words. If the feeling was a colour, what colour would it be? Most of the sensations I registered were pain-related. But the more I saw the trauma masseuse, the more I noticed that my body was in a constant state of flux. Sensations of all types came and went in waves. In time, under her gentle guidance, I got better at learning to sit with them. If trauma, no matter what kind, no matter the cause, could freeze us in a state of disassociation or disembodiment — a state of being that made connection with sensation difficult — perhaps it was through relearning to inhabit the body that the aftereffects of trauma might be mitigated?

My mother has always been drawn to complicated or difficult men. When she approved of a new man in my life, she was probably thinking, Ooh, he looks like a bit of hard work. How delightful! I'd learned to take my mother's endorsement of a potential love interest as something of a red flag. I wondered what she would think of this older man. Worryingly, I suspected she would find him appealing.

Since the man's first email about getting a drink, I'd developed an ongoing case of conjunctivitis, mixed with several flus and a nasty chest infection. Before meeting him, I hadn't been sick in years. Conjunctivitis was a new thing. My eyes were giving me trouble. Both the doctor and the optometrist said it was an idiosyncratic case. Afraid I had some terrifying immune disorder, I went to the ophthalmologist, who pronounced that my 'tear film' was malfunctioning. Tear film — the protective layer of moistness that coats your eyes when you blink — was made up of a delicate blend of substances that sometimes got out of balance. The phrase 'tear film' was oddly poetic and I tried not to think about how mine was now full of holes. I tried not to think of how many tears I'd shed. The ophthalmologist told me to drink more water and sit tight. As I waited for my body to calm, I hoped the older man wouldn't forget me.

More than anything, the new Koolie pup, Tully, liked to try catching sticks, 'try' being the operative word. He stared intently at the stick in my hand and, when I threw it, launched himself into the air for the catch, twisting, somersaulting, often landing in a loose pile of askew limbs. He never caught the stick. It was easy to laugh at his efforts — all his wild exertion, his blatant lack of skill — but his pleasure in the game was unflagging. I wondered what it would be like to be so removed from any sense of failure. To find so much joy in the trying. To throw my body around with so much effort and so little grace. To be so unashamed of the outcome. The new pup wasn't trying to teach me anything, but I was learning.

~

When I first met the older man and felt those concentric circles and wondered if they had some meaning, I knew deep down that I would try to find out. Watching my body panic with the lack of safety, there was a part of me — through the conjunctivitis and chest infections and the general unravelling — that cried out, can't I just bypass the whole thing?

I laid my head on the table at a local writer friend's house, closing my eyes in defeat.

'Can't I just skip the shitty relationship and go straight to the writing about it after?' I asked softly.

'Oh, love, the only way is through,' she said, a gentle hand on my shoulder.

I sat up straight, rubbed a hand over my dark constricted heart, shook myself off and went home. I booked my flight to his city, then emailed him to tell him I was coming.

The only way was through.

passionfruit

When I finally emailed the older man to say I was going to be in his city, he wrote straight back — 'I am free every night you are here, just let me know what suits.' I took this as a good sign. My tongue began swelling in anticipation. I had one trick up my sleeve when it came to my recalcitrant body — a beta-blocker. Writing my novels had required me to talk publicly about them, a task I found incompatible with general existence. In everyday life there was nothing I enjoyed more than talking, but ever since I was a child I'd baulked at any kind of performative or public speaking. I wasn't overcome with anxious thoughts, my body simply refused to cooperate. I came out in hives, I twitched and shuddered. I displayed strange, compulsive behaviours like twirling my clothes into balls and rubbing my belly. Even if my words sounded coherent enough, my body screamed 'freak show!' Nothing I tried contained it. When the publication of my first novel drew close, I began to panic. A GP prescribed me Valium, but it did nothing, or made matters worse. I read that a high percentage of orchestra members took beta-blockers to suppress nerves and body tremors. The GP was sceptical, but he wrote me a prescription. And boom! One beta-blocker pre–public speaking and the semblance of normality returned.

—

The day I arrived in the city, the man sent me an email saying, 'I have been trying to call you, but the number I have doesn't seem to work, can you call me please?' The 'please' seemed too frantic or pushy to my phone-phobic ears. My chest tightened, my heart-beat pounded at my temples. The idea that the older man had been trying to call me, rather than just texting or emailing, was terrifying enough, but that I was required to make that first call — me who had been avoiding all spoken phone contact with strangers for more than two decades — was almost a bridge too far. I'd come all this way to see what might be between us, but would a phone call make the next steps impossible? I was staying with a friend, but I hadn't told her anything about my poten-tial meeting with the older man. While she pottered around preparing dinner, I yelled 'fuck, fuck, fuck' in my head on repeat, then excused myself, stepped out onto the street and dialled his number. He sounded comfortable, in his element, bordering on smooth. I don't know how I could have sounded anything but petrified.

—

Before our proposed drink, I met up with my brother at a cafe near his work. I was to catch up with the older man later in the evening. My brother had always radiated calm, and I felt sure that just being in his presence would help settle my jangled nerves.

We sat down together and I took in his face — his kind eyes, the new grey in his beard. We'd always looked similar, brown eyes, brown hair, recognisably siblings. Sometimes when we met up at a cafe in his city the waitress would assume we were on a date and treat us like awkward new lovers. Once that assumption had been made, it was hard to undo. 'He's my brother,' I'd want to say. 'I haven't seen him in a while.' But in the city, you didn't need to explain your relationships to waitstaff you'd never see again, so I restrained myself from speaking.

We ordered teas, and we chatted about his life, but I was having trouble concentrating on his answers.

'So, who is this guy again?' he asked, as though I'd explained and he had forgotten. 'You seem a little on edge?'

'Just this person I met a while back.' I shrugged. There was no way I was telling anyone about the concentric circles.

We sipped our teas, and sat in almost silence, as was my brother's custom. Being with him was soothing, but before long it was time to go. My brother hugged me goodbye on the street.

'Good luck,' he said, watching my face carefully, thinking his secret thoughts.

As I set off to meet the older man, I popped my beta-blocker. I couldn't do much to stop my tongue from swelling, but I could at least turn up without coming out in hives. Despite our six months of emailing, I'd convinced myself that our meeting was not a date, but that the older man was just impeccably polite, fulfilling the terms of his earlier invitation. Perhaps this was now an irritating duty? It was six months since I'd met him, what if I was wrong about the circles?

He was waiting for me in a booth near the door of the pub. I saw him before he saw me. He had ditched the suit of our first meeting and was wearing jeans and an old soft shirt. Head down, peering at his phone, he looked serene. As I shuffled into the booth, he glanced up, and right away I was enveloped in an aura of warmth. I'd needed the beta-blocker to get there, but maybe I hadn't needed it in his company. He had his own beta-blocking powers. We chatted about our kids, he had sons a few years older than mine, and it was easy, the kind of easy I wouldn't expect with a virtual stranger. I am often attracted to people who can put me at ease. I experience them as a kind of medicine, soothing to my inflamed nervous system, like a calming cup of tea. But there was something else there, I suspected, a subtle undercurrent of mutual attraction.

'I'm terrible with women,' he stated, a few beers in.

I sat up straighter.

A confession.

He talked me through his history blow-by-blow. I have a friend who hates people disclosing their relationship ineptitude upfront. She claims that, although the honesty is beguiling, they only share about it early so that when they treat you badly later on, they can say that you were warned. A get-out-of-jail-free card, she calls it. I could see her point, but that night I was watching for multiple flags, the most pressing one being — in what way is he interested in me? So, though I was listening intently to the description of his past relationships, storing the information away for future pondering, I was also struck by the fact that he was telling me at all.

This is a date! I thought, with some surprise.

We had a couple more drinks and then walked up the street to an old-school Italian restaurant, where the waiter hovered unnecessarily.

Once we'd ordered, and the waiter had moved away, I asked the man how old he was.

'Sixty, just,' he said. 'How old are you?'

'Thirty-eight,' I said.

His face pinkened, and I realised he'd thought I was older. No one ever thought I was older. I wondered if it was the age of my kids, if he hadn't factored in how young I'd been when I had them.

He took a sip of water. 'That's young,' he said, once he'd swallowed.

'Yes, but my hair is totally grey. I dye it.' An odd admission. Was I trying to help him regain his footing?

'I'm losing mine,' he said. 'Sometimes I look in the mirror and don't recognise myself.'

I glanced at his hair, but I'd already noticed it was thinning.

'All the men who were important to me were dead by the time they were sixty,' I blurted. As soon as the words were out of my mouth, I wished I could retrieve them. Press rewind, then delete.

Thankfully, I was saved by the arrival of the food and wine.

He'd ordered gnocchi with chilli, and sweat was forming on his forehead. I hoped it wasn't my statement about all the dead men.

After dinner we walked around the streets for a bit, then stopped at another pub for a few more drinks. He looked around and said, 'I am the oldest person here, by a good twenty years.'

I shrugged in agreement.

Having no experience of one-night-stands, pubs or dates, or how I might initiate moving from a public sphere to a private one, I was relying on him to make the move. He looked defeated.

'I'm getting tired,' he said. 'I think I'll have to go soon.'

I jumped up from my seat.

'No hurry,' he said gently.

I'd been relaxed but, abruptly, I was alert. Goodbyes were often fraught for me: my body wanted to run. That night, I tried to repress the impulse, to fight the feeling of impending doom. I hoped my disappointment wasn't showing. I'd fought six months of conjunctivitis to get here! Thus far, with the help of beta-blockers, I'd had a twitch-free night! I didn't want it to end. I looked at him, his narrow face littered with life-lines, and I thought, what is it about you? Twenty years older, slightly melancholic. What is it about you that has caught my interest? The circles had not reappeared, but there was his aura of warm generosity.

The night was over. He helped me into a taxi. I felt dazed all the way back to my friend's house.

'It was a date!' I said, when she opened the door for me.

'What makes you so sure?'

'Just the feel of it.'

Sleepy-eyed, she wandered back to bed.

I wanted to sleep with him, but I didn't know why.

~

Back home in the forest, I was flying high on my success. I hadn't spun around on the spot or twirled my clothes or twitched. I'd conversed with a seemingly sensible man about all manner of things. I'd sat in a pub (two pubs!) in a relatively foreign city. I'd eaten at a restaurant, managed to swallow the food. I'd made a fucking phone call! It had taken a beta-blocker to get to the date, but I might not have needed it. There were no concentric circles, but there was very possibly *something*. He didn't always wear a suit. He lived two thousand kilometres away, but I was definitely going back.

~

The next time I visited his city he asked me to dinner at his house. His dog was very old and sick and it was hard for him to leave it. When I explained about the old dog to the friend I was staying with, she smiled.

'It's a sex-thing,' she said. 'It's always a sex-thing when they ask you to their house.'

I felt my tongue swell instantly. My body started up its twitching.

'Is it?' I was in unfamiliar territory.

She nodded, like the wise woman she was.

The prospect of his warmth didn't stop me taking a beta-blocker. I was going to need fortification.

I knocked, bringing nothing, and he welcomed me inside. He had intimated that his house was decrepit, but it was the nicest house I'd been inside in that city. Even with the beta-blocker I was nervous. He had recipe books out and was preparing what looked like a fancy dinner. A salmon curry with several sides. The old dog was large and sheep-doggy and didn't register my presence. The man I desired offered me wine, which I accepted. He continued cooking and chatting while I wondered how I would know if it was a sex-thing or not.

After dinner (I ate a few mouthfuls) we retired to the loungeroom and sat on the couch, both staring at the old dog, who lay on a dog mat in the centre of the room. Disorientated, the dog was facing away from our attention. Occasionally, the man patted him fondly, calling him by name. We listened to some music, some alt country band I'd never heard of, and we talked. It was getting late and I was unsure if I should leave.

'Let me know if it's time to go,' I said in confusion. 'I don't know when the last tram leaves.'

He shrugged, 'It's okay. You can always stay here. I have a spare room.'

He looked unworried, but the mention of the spare room

troubled me. Did he think he was some gentle, uncle-like figure? Perhaps this wasn't a date at all?

Politeness was not something I encountered much in the forest. He was by far the most dapper, sophisticated, polite man I'd ever come across. How was I to read him?

I moved closer to him on the couch. He did not seem to register it, though I wondered at his stillness. Was there a receptivity in it? We'd had wine and a little whisky and now we were onto a cup of tea. I was slightly tipsy, but nothing serious.

The dog staggered up, and the man I desired staggered up too.

'Oh no!' he muttered, whipping a plastic bag from his back pocket and pulling it open. The dog was about to shit right there on the carpet.

'Oh dear,' he murmured, flustered. He caught the shit expertly in the plastic bag, then tied it up and ducked outside to the bin, glancing across at me apologetically. The dog circled, then lay back down on the mat. I could hear the man washing his hands in the bathroom. When he came back, he looked chagrined, caught out.

'Sometimes he doesn't make it outside.'

I'd gathered that.

Something in the man's demeanour had changed, as though the promise of seduction had been wiped out with the dog shit, as though now he could truly relax. He sat back down on the couch and I shuffled closer. I know a dog shitting isn't sexy, but the vulnerability of the man in that moment, clutching the plastic bag, his murmured 'oh dear', gave me spirit. I shuffled as close as I could be without touching him. He remained as placid as a lake. I was a stormy sea. I wanted to sleep with him, even though he'd just caught dog shit in mid-air with a plastic bag clearly kept in his back pocket for that express purpose. Despite the beta-blocker, my skin was beginning to tingle all over. Would he ever invite me to his house again? Was this my only chance?

I launched into a story about the last man who'd tried to court me. Speedy Dave, a hermit from down the road who lived in an unfinished house made only of doors. Recently, as he drove past, he'd seen me gardening and had popped in to have a look. Speedy Dave was of indeterminate age, but had been an adult all my life, so was significantly older than me. For reasons that remained unexplained, he was wearing an eye patch that day and had a bandaid on his cheek. I'd known him as long as I remembered, but I saw straightaway that I'd come suddenly to his notice, and I knew he would come back again to see me. Sure enough, he turned up the next day for a visit, but I wouldn't come out of the house. There was no way I was giving an iota of encouragement to Speedy Dave.

'Yes, well, it's hard to meet people, I find,' the man I desired said mildly. 'I wonder who my version of Speedy Dave is?'

I was on the precipice of an abyss. I was about to throw myself over.

'Have you ever thought about me in that way?' I said, trying to hold his gaze.

'What way?' He seemed bewildered.

I was suddenly drowning.

'As someone you might like to …' I stumbled to a halt, all the heat in my body rising to my face.

He stared at me, visibly shocked.

'Oh no,' he stuttered. 'No, no.'

My heart dived steeply, a roller-coaster drop.

'No, no, no.' He glanced down at his hands for a moment, then back up at me, as if he was struggling to find the right words. 'I mean, it's not that I haven't thought about it. I have.'

And there it was, at least, an acknowledgement of desire.

'It's just … no, no.'

I hung my head, the humiliation overwhelming.

I need to leave, I thought. Now.

'Oh oh, are you sad?' he said, sounding concerned. He reached out and patted my head, like I was a child.

'I'm so, so embarrassed.'

'It's just, I don't think,' he paused, 'I want that kind of complication in my life.' He seemed to consider it a little more. 'No, no. I don't.'

'I've missed the last tram.' I wanted to curl up in a ball and cry.

'Oh, that's okay. You can sleep in the spare bed.' He got up. 'I'll just get some fresh sheets.'

I followed him into the spare room and helped him pull the sheets tight. Maybe it was a gentle-uncle thing? My cheeks were still burning, but the all-consuming feeling of failure was lessening. It is okay, I reassured myself. You will survive this. He is kind and you have committed no crime. When he leaves you here, you can cry by yourself.

It wasn't a sex-thing after all.

The man I desired went to fetch some extra blankets. Alone in the spare room, I was surprised by a sudden burst of elation. You did it, I told myself. You tried! And suddenly it didn't seem that bad at all. What could be worse than this? Nothing! And even this isn't bad. You aren't even blushing anymore. You've ridden the humiliation like a wave and now you are ashore!

I walked out of the spare room smiling and almost bumped into him. We stood in the hallway, looking at each other. I was still high on the adrenaline of failure.

'We are both adults, aren't we?' he asked tentatively.

I'd lived thirty-eight years in the forest. I knew I lacked sophistication. I understood why he might think of me as child-like, but I was approaching forty, almost middle-aged.

'My children are nearly grown-ups,' I said.

'I know that. But it's impossible for me to imagine.'

'We're both adults.' I confirmed. 'And really, it's not that complicated.'

In truth, I knew nothing about the complications of casual sex, but I was willing to believe it was possibly not that complicated in the right circumstances. Were these the right circumstances?

I set about straightening the books on the shelves in the hall. Not even the beta-blocker could contain this nervous tic. He stood there watching me.

'Well,' he hesitated, 'maybe we could cuddle?' he said.

'Spooning?' I almost whooped. 'Spooning is the best part!'

I wanted to skip down that hallway.

'Can you give me something else to wear?' I did not want to spoon in my dress.

It turned out he had drawers of pyjamas, all soft and worn. He handed me a set, but I only took the bottoms. If I rolled them up five times they would fit. He was very tall and slim and I was short and curved. He offered me a T-shirt, but the ugliness of the shirt felt a step too far.

'I'm right,' I said looking down at the skivvy I was wearing under my dress. I pulled off my bra, slipping the straps out from under my skivvy, breathing a sigh of relief. Freedom from constraint.

Spooning is better than nothing, I thought happily, as I climbed into his bed.

He went to check on the old dog one last time and then climbed in beside me, looking faintly startled. He leaned across and kissed me on the lips, just a peck, like a tester. I was thrown. I'd settled into the idea of cuddling, but this was something else.

'Really?' I asked.

He shrugged, then kissed me again. I hoped he didn't notice my swollen tongue. How would I go about explaining that?

We are both adults, I thought. Stay with this.

Even though I'd attempted to initiate it, the whole thing caught me by surprise. He touched me like a man who knows how to touch women. Like a man who was used to paying attention to women's bodies. Like a man who had taken note. I have never been touched like this, I thought. Is that sad? What has my life even been? Stay with it, I told myself again. Stay with him.

Up until this moment, my older man had been a touch reserved, terribly polite and impeccably clean, but now naked, he was all confidence, precision, and presence. As though he was bringing his whole self to this moment, while my thoughts were darting about like spooked sheep in a storm. I was trying to herd them into the yard, but one or more of them would keep escaping. He's so good at this! Concentrate! Should I be doing more? What should I be doing? Be in your body!

Even that first time he said my name like an incantation. All his focus was on me! I realised that in my past there had always been others in the room: the men I'd slept with had closed their eyes to me and thought their private thoughts. They hadn't been with me the way he was, and I struggled to meet him there. And all the while the beta-blocker kept my heartbeat from quickening, so no matter how expert his touch, I couldn't come. And I couldn't say to him, it's the medication I took to stop me looking crazy, because that would sound crazy, and my biggest fear was appearing crazy. Even without the orgasm, it was the best sex I'd had.

'What are you thinking?' I asked him as we lay quietly.

'What a lovely surprise you are,' he said. 'This is.'

'What do you mean?'

'Well, I just … didn't see it coming.'

I wanted to say how I was surprised too, but mainly by how good a lover he was. But that seemed like a backhanded compliment, so I kept it to myself.

I didn't sleep all night, my nervous system so aroused, my excitement so heightened, I couldn't bring it down. I lay still beside him, trying not to disturb him, and when we got up in the morning, I snuck off to take another beta-blocker because I was close to weeping with fatigue and frayed nerves, and my body was beginning to shake all over. It's all going to come tumbling down if I don't get my body in hand, I thought. I'd never had a one-night stand and had no idea about the protocol the next morning. How long was I supposed to hang around? Wild with adrenaline, I couldn't eat more than a teaspoon of yoghurt and muesli.

'I guess I better go,' I piped up in fear.

'I will walk you to your tram,' he said, unruffled.

Out in the sunshine, he was back to his gentlemanly self. I was fighting flashes of his expert hand between my legs. I hoped it wasn't showing on my face.

A friend of his was waiting at the tram stop too, and we chatted, or they did. I tried to inhabit a space where this was normal. Standing at a tram stop with the man I desired, talking about the weather with another older man. When the tram came, my one-night stand surprised me by kissing me on the mouth to say goodbye, while his friend smirked next to us. We got on the tram together, his friend and I. He sat away from me, but I could tell he was keeping me in his sights. When I got off at my stop he waved and smiled, and I imagined him thinking, well, some blokes have all the luck. Even knowing I'd projected the thought, I still felt pleased.

Romantic relationships had always seemed a mystery to me. Everyone else understood how to behave, but I simply didn't. It was as though that part of my brain was impaired. Rebuilding it took a consistent daily effort, like a form of rehabilitation. I was trying to forge new neural pathways and regenerate damaged nerves. I was trying to reanimate my ability to trust. The process was infinitesimally slow. I'd never had this trouble in my relationships with women. I was still close with my girlfriends from high school — those shiny shiny girls — and after my books had been published, I'd collected new female friends without too much fuss. Rarely did we get into a kerfuffle. Rarely did we misunderstand. Not to say there wasn't emotional labour keeping up these female friendships, or times when perhaps one of us leant on the other too hard. But, usually, once a crisis passed, so too did the extra leaning. For me, equilibrium was easily found within my female friendships, and there wasn't much of a tussle to get there.

~

A week after I returned home, I received a book in the post from the older man. A book of photographs — an illustrated history — of an ageing popstar he knew I liked. No card or note, just the older man's name on the back of the package. It was something I would do, sending a gift to a new lover. It smacked of keenness, but, in this case, the keenness seemed tempered by the lack of note. It gave me a thrill to receive it, but I wasn't sure how to respond. A few days passed and there was an email in my inbox, "Did you get my parcel?' Slightly anxious, as though he was worried the gift was lost in the post. 'I got it!' I wrote back quickly, ashamed of my hesitation. 'Thank you, it's great!'

~

Most Friday nights, I stayed at Nika's house. My closest friend, geographically, Nika lived about forty minutes' drive away, but really it was just a few hills over. I lived in a valley, and she lived high in the mountains. Just seeing the vista from her house made my heart lift. I met Nika in Year Nine when I changed schools and she was assigned to take me under her wing. She struck me as the most boy-crazy girl I'd ever met, manic with love for her crush, chatting about him endlessly with wild-eyed zeal. I was interested in boys, but not with that degree of fixation. Nearly thirty years later, I had come to see that Nika and I were far more similar than I realised back then. Over the years we'd fallen into a habit of joint ruminating. Together we would discuss the particulars of the situation with whoever we'd fallen for. Both of us could go for ages without a crush, but we also took years to get over the last one. There was always a lot to talk about, but mostly it was soothing, even fun.

As I had no reception in the forest, I occasionally texted with the older man on Friday night at Nika's. Convivial chit-chat, different from our emails. One night he called me. I stared at his name on the screen in horror, but I answered. He said my name in a way that made me feel he longed for me — I was sure in that instant he felt as I did.

'So, when will we do it again?' The words popped from my mouth.

I sensed his panic on the end of the line. Maybe he didn't expect me to be so direct? I didn't expect to be so direct.

'Oh no,' he said, as he had that first night. 'I don't think that's what I want.'

I was shocked into silence, as if I'd been enveloped in ice.

'You see, I don't think I want the complication of it.' That word again.

I felt drained. It was like a punch to the solar plexus.

'Are you alright?' he asked gently. I tried to force myself to form words.

'I'm just disappointed,' I said, weakly. 'I'm alright.'

His ambivalence hit me like a speeding train.

Oh no! I moaned. I've done it again.

I couldn't tell Nika that night. I couldn't tell anyone.

—

Approaching forty, I could look back over previous romantic relationships and see some patterns. Heterosexuality, thus far, was my sexual preference. Despite rarely leaving the forest, I'd managed to have a few relationships with blokes since breaking up with the father of my sons. Each one had been ambivalent, from either their perspective or mine. I always assumed there were basic things we agreed on about falling in love, or falling in lust, but maybe that wasn't true. For instance, I was never attracted to men who came on strong in the beginning. I found them so sexually unappealing it was hard to imagine that other people didn't react in the same way. My distaste felt innate, like a truth we must all share. But I watched other friends be 'swept off their feet' by the kind of intense behaviour that would alienate me in an instant.

I knew, of course, that all individuals had unique patterns of desire, but how much of this patterning was influenced by our prior experiences, and how much of it was part of our so-called makeup? The degree to which I seemed to require ambivalence in order to feel sexually interested or aroused was, frankly, unhealthy. It was as though my neural pathways — love-lines — only fired up under those very particular conditions. I recognised the problem but couldn't change it. I'd tried to be with people who were keener on me than I found appealing, but it never ended well.

—

The kindest and keenest boyfriend I'd had came into my life in my mid-thirties, while recovering from a gruelling four-year ambivalent relationship. My nervous system was in tatters. For the first time in my life, I had completely broken down. I went to a psychiatrist and started taking antidepressants. When I met this kind man, I intuited his keenness and felt instantaneously that I would never reciprocate. But I had come to be suspicious of my patterns of desire and their usefulness. What was the point of only being attracted to those who were ambivalent about me? Where did it lead? As far as I was concerned, nowhere good. Why not give this kind, keen man a go? I did not actively pursue his company, but I let him pursue mine. He was reliable. He was nurturing. It had been a long time since I'd been loved, and my nervous system began to repair. I stopped taking the anti-depressants. I plumped up with the care. I liked to sleep with this man, I enjoyed his touch, but I never felt deeply about him. I wasn't in love. Not even close. The first time we spoke about our discrepancy in feeling, he was so shocked he wept. But I'd never promised that I'd be anything other than willing and happy to be in his company. I told him as carefully as I could that I didn't think my feelings for him would grow, and I let him decide what he was willing to live with. We were together for eighteen months, and they were among the most contented months of my life. He broke up with me, of course, hoping to find someone who could truly love him, and I wished him well.

Even though he had nurtured me back to wellness with his care and devotion, I did not miss him, not even for one day. And yes, I did wonder what was wrong with me, to be so cavalier with another's love. That time, it was my ambivalence that got in the way, but, in truth, ambivalence seems too strong a word. I liked that man. I respected him. I offered him care and I was free with my body. But there was nothing flickering inside me. Would it always be that way? Could my love-lines not be moved?

What was it about the asymmetry of desire that seemed to fan it? Was it something that was blatantly obvious to everyone but me? I consulted my friend Brad, whom I'd met at a writers' house when I first left the forest. He was younger than me and intuitive about love. When I was in the grips of my four years of ambivalent-love-hell he served as my lifeline. After the older man's rejection, I begged Brad's forgiveness for being so terribly unteachable, and asked him, via email, to explain to me again why I always fell so hard for those who were unsure about me.

As I knew he would, he wrote to me about my father and about abandonment. He wrote about wounds that my body-self was trying to resolve. Intellectually, I understood that if your father committed suicide when you were on the cusp of adulthood, your experience of love and loyalty and dependability might become troubled. But I found it difficult to properly absorb. Was it the trauma itself, making everything foggy? Whenever I tried to think clearly about my experience, I felt I was swimming through oil. The synapses didn't fire, there was a strange cognitive lag. I was reading Brad's words, but I couldn't seem to comprehend them. He did make one suggestion that penetrated the fog.

'Why don't you experiment with doing the opposite of what you would usually do?'

I thought about this. I thought about it a lot.

What I would usually do when faced with the ambivalence of my desired lover:

Panic. Cry. Fret. Exercise excessively to curb anxiety. Try to supress the desire. Withdraw. Cuddle dog too hard. Talk in circles to Nika. Try to stop talking. Keep things to myself. Break down and reach out to the object of my desire in order to be soothed. Experience more ambivalence. Cue the cycle starting again.

It's true, it wasn't pretty.

So, step one in doing the opposite: don't panic.

—

How to stop panicking? Examine what it was I was panicking about. Of course, I'd tried this before. I am, by nature, an analytical, reflective person, but panic doesn't leave much room for ordered thinking. I'd found that chanting to myself, please don't panic, please don't panic, like a mantra, in an attempt to find the headspace to examine the panic, didn't do much good. Instead, I went through a number of reality checks.

How long have you known this man? Not very long.

Were you okay before you met him? Yes, at that point I was content.

If he disappeared from your life now, would it be any different? Probably not.

If you never saw him again, would you survive? Undoubtedly.

After going through the questions repeatedly, I felt calmer, which gave me space to reflect. Did I perceive my one-time lover's ambivalence as a threat to my happy existence? To do so would be kind of nuts since I'd existed without this man for most of my life. Progress! And yet I started to feel a kind of sickness swell in my belly because I sensed, like a scent on the wind, that I was about to come up against something I intensely disliked to think about.

Worthiness.

Specifically, my own.

How to come at such a nausea-inducing word? I liked to believe that I was alright with worthiness. That I chose to stay in the forest simply because I liked it there. In the forest I received the undimming affection of my mother and children and all the plants and pets (only an occasional growl from the dog). There was no one else there to test that reality. Worthiness was not a concern.

Was I that deluded?

When I fell into lust with someone who was ambivalent about me, the sense of my own worthiness — so unshakeable in the forest — dissolved. Often, I also understood that the ambivalent party had issues of their own: a long history of problems with commitment, a damaged relationship with their mother. Abandonment! Abandonment! Abandonment! But knowing the other person's possible shortcomings did nothing to curb the rapid loss of my sense of worth.

In the worst case of ambivalent love I'd experienced, the four years of unrequited-love-hell, I began to despise myself with an unprecedented force. I would get in the bath at night in an attempt to self-soothe and spend the whole time looking down on my poor, long-suffering body thinking, I hate you, I hate you,

I hate you, like some kind of demented dirge. I fought the urge to cut into the skin on my arms, like a desolate teenage girl, to inflict some punishment on myself. I never did cut myself, but I understood the need to. I craved the feeling of relief that I imagined it would provide. That man seemed to enjoy my desire for him, despite not returning it. Whenever I got close to breaking free from his orbit, he would reel me back in, so I was caught in an unending cycle of hope and rejection. To get out I had to insist he never contact me again.

It's telling, how he responded —

'But I get so much from our interaction.'

Broken, psychologically battered, taking antidepressants I had never previously needed, three dress sizes smaller, a shell of who I was before we met, I looked across at him and spoke the words I needed to, 'No more.'

Revisiting this memory, it struck me that I might be panicking about the degree of self-destruction my last experience of love involved. How to give away your life-force in 1400 days. This time around, could I be trusted to take care of myself?

⁓

The older man's dog was ailing. He couldn't decide when to put him out of his misery. He made an appointment, then wavered. Made an appointment, then wavered. Finally, he didn't waver. I felt his desolation through his Friday-night text message. I sent him my condolences. I knew what it was like to love a dog.

Following Brad's advice, I'd toned down my panic enough to examine its cause. Abandonment (yes!), belief in unworthiness (hurray!). Thus far I had not cried. Brooding was a given. I'd exercised to minimise anxiety, but not excessively. And yes, I'd hugged the dog a little harder than necessary, but I had not descended into hell. Things were looking up.

The older man and I messaged from time to time, though nothing significant was said.

I had to admit, I liked that the older man was ambivalent. It was probably not a stretch to say it turned me on. What would happen if I tried to accept that part of myself? If I tried to accommodate it? No longer raged at myself for being wrongheaded in my desires. What if I stopped aiming for certainty about love from someone I desired, most likely, because they were unable to be certain? What if I simply aimed to explore?

Maybe I was a glutton for punishment, but I kept remembering how he'd said my name, so filled with longing. As I walked in the forest, a passionfruit fell at my feet. Fell from what felt like the sky. I looked down at it — brown and ordinary on the outside but moist and delicious inside — and I thought, I am that passionfruit, falling into his world, and he is refusing to eat me. We will both be dead soon. He is a fool. I sent him a photo of the passionfruit in the post and a note to tell him of his folly.

You idiot! I feel you shout. You must listen to what men tell you about themselves. He was frank. Let it go!

But I didn't. I booked a flight, told him I was coming, and waited (anxiously, yes) to see what he would do.

~

About an hour after I arrived at my friend's house in town, I received a text from him: 'Welcome back. How was your flight?'

That's keen, I thought. How nice.

He rang me soon after and we arranged a date. I'd made a pact with myself that there would be no beta-blockers, because this time I wanted my heartbeat to be able to fly. And if he was going to touch me in his masterful way, I wanted to be able to respond properly, but that meant I was in a bit of a pickle about my expressive body. Keep it together, I whispered to myself, but I already felt the beginnings of the tremors.

On the way over to his place on the tram I concentrated on breathing, and focused — as my trauma masseuse had instructed — on the sensation of my feet on the ground. I'd used my last book advance to pay for those trauma-massage sessions. The money was gone now, so I no longer saw her, but I remembered what she'd said. I breathed as evenly as I could to avoid the possibility of hyperventilating. I hadn't started shaking, so things were going pretty well.

When I got to his place, he welcomed me with surprising warmth for someone who did not wish to have sex again. I noted, somewhat gleefully, when it came to wanting to see me, he didn't always mean what he said. We pottered about, then we went to see a film and on to a restaurant. Back home, he offered me a glass of wine and we sat on the couch. All that time, my body held firm, but there on the couch, I started twitching. Not wildly, but enough that he noticed.

'What's going on here?' he asked, motioning to my shoulder.

'I just … It's just … sometimes that happens.'

He took a sip of wine and watched me, a gentle gaze.

'Well, that's alright.' He stretched his arm along the couch behind me, almost an embrace. 'We'll just let it settle.'

My desire flared up fiercely then, my mouth felt full of marbles. I twitched a little more and tried not to feel ashamed.

He got up to put on some music and we listened to it, perhaps slightly too loud.

'I can't turn it down,' he said. 'It's stuck at that volume.'

I'd gone from twitching to full-body tremors. I wanted to say, this is how my body does desire. I wanted to say, soothe me. I wanted to say, come on! But I didn't. He sipped his wine and I sipped mine. He sat close to me on the couch and he didn't seem disturbed by my trembling. I tried not to be disturbed either.

Finally it all got too much and I climbed onto his lap.

He said my name, my full name, and I felt it then, all of his desire in those two words, and my body shook and shook, and he squeezed me as though he was trying to hold me still, but I knew it wouldn't work.

I didn't bother to try to explain. I kissed him instead. He wasn't so ambivalent that he didn't kiss me back. And then his hands were on me and my body flew and flew.

'Come to bed,' he whispered, and I skipped down the hallway, wonky and off-centre, but happy that my twitching didn't seem to matter.

I liked that his fingers knew all my secret places and that he never touched me tentatively, but with confidence. He would put his fingers anywhere — in my mouth, in my arse, twined in my hair — and he would ask, do you like that? The sensations so new, so overwhelming, I often didn't know. If I couldn't answer, he tried to read my body like braille, measuring my shuddery breaths. That time we fucked I didn't feel sad for myself and all the pleasures I'd never known. Even with the trembling and all the marbles in my mouth, I came like a bursting river bank and he laughed and I watched his belly ripple.

He went to boil the kettle.

'Sex and a cup of tea,' he said. 'My favourite kind of day.'

~

Before sleeping with this man, I'd never delved into the subject of older men with younger women. It seemed boring. So many clichés, so many centuries of tedious examples. Everywhere in our culture the phenomenon stared back at me. I'd dismissed it with a mixture of, 'yeah, yuck' and 'each to their own'. I'd never desired older men. My father, though disastrous in his spectacular way, did not leave me with that specific void to fill. With pointed rancour, I'd despised older men who made passes at me. They seemed so deluded, assuming their desire might be shared. I decided that older men were incapable of reflection, so stranded in their own perspectives they found it impossible to imagine themselves from the outside. I hated the way they talked at me with the assumption that I was interested and they were interesting, both things being patently untrue. Occasionally, one particular friend of my father's would call me on the landline in the forest and commence talking at me with barely even a hello. He could talk for forty minutes straight without any encouragement. I knew he was lonely, but his pure, unbridled selfishness raised my hackles. I would put the phone down on the counter and leave him talking to himself. I knew what it was like to need to be heard, but I hadn't been able to extend my compassion to include him.

But the man I desired did not, as far as I could see, display this delusion or selfishness. He never talked at me. He listened to my words carefully. He often apologised for talking about himself just when I wanted to know more about him. He did not take my interest for granted. He did not presume that he was interesting. He was gentle with my nervousness, gave it space. Why do younger women sleep with older men? Access to their power, their authority? Access to their wealth? Perhaps the women have been manipulated? Perhaps they are taking advantage? Why do older men sleep with younger women? Because there is an imbalance of power they can exploit? Because being in proximity to youth and beauty boosts their flagging egos? I wondered about the wives of older men who had been discarded, and what they had been discarded for. An upgrade. The latest model. All I had were these simplistic stereotypes I'd semi-believed, because I'd never felt any desire in that direction.

Somewhere in the midst of those early hook-ups, the man I desired said, 'I don't want to be taking advantage of you.'

It was clear he was grappling, just as I had been.

'What do you mean?' I said, though I already knew.

'Just the age difference.'

I narrowed my eyes. 'Are you talking about power?'

The problem is, as they say, as old as time.

'No, no,' he stuttered. And in that moment the suggestion did seem ludicrous. I'd made him lie on the carpeted floor beside me, a place I liked to be, and he — a bit stiff — clearly did not.

'Because when you say that, it's as if I have no agency. As if I am unable to choose.'

He shuffled uncomfortably beside me. The hard ground probably hurt his back.

'I just don't want to be taking advantage,' he said again, trying to sound resolute.

I lifted my hand to touch his face. The lines and crevices were becoming lovely to me.

'We are both adults,' I said. 'Remember.'

And I saw he wouldn't fight it, even if he suspected there was still something deeply worrying about it.

—

Our culture told us two very different stories about adulthood. Firstly, that there was one person out there who would 'complete' us, and our mission was to find that person and live happily ever after. This story ran parallel to the second story: independence was our primary aim, to be 'adult' meant being self-sufficient. Dependency in adulthood was frowned upon unless it was dependency on that person with whom we have formed a romantic attachment, the person who completes us. What a precarious way to live!

It had been a long time since I'd fantasied about romantic love as the basis for family. After creating a family with my high-school boyfriend and seeing it disintegrate, much like my family of origin, I had lost faith that it was through desire and falling in love that we found security or completeness or peace. For me, being in love had always been accompanied by dramatic highs and lows, constant intrusive thinking, excessive unhelpful fantasising, as well as bouts of uncharacteristic anxiety and depression. All of these symptoms felt involuntary and destabilising. Studies had showed the brains of people who identified as being in love lit up in the same way as those of cocaine addicts, and there was also significant crossover in brain chemistry with dysfunctions such as obsessive-compulsive disorder. I grudgingly accepted that I had a propensity towards experiencing this state, but I tried to avoid making important life decisions around it. It seemed odd that our culture should lionise a state of being so obviously psychologically difficult. The highs of falling in love were, of course, high, but the lows were hard to bear. There was very little evidence in the world around me that relationships based on desire or falling in love had the kind of solidity required to raise children or create homes. I wondered how our culture had constructed the myth that desire was a firm foundation to build other dreams.

~

When the man I desired slept with me, he held me close afterwards.

'We will do this, and when we can't, we will be good friends,' he whispered.

He said this like an affirmation.

Sometimes I wanted to say, there's no reason we can't do this forever, but then I'd think, well, forever is a long time. Who knew what would happen tomorrow? Longstanding friendship was a good end goal. What a promise, I thought. After this, we will be good friends.

~

Long-distance relationships are often seen as doomed. Either because the interest might wane, or because no home is being created. There's also the issue of uneven needs, of jealousy, of suspicion. Of being unable to allay these fears without the physical presence of the one you desire. Those issues did not outweigh my enjoyment of the sporadic nature of our meetings. I wasn't interested in marriage, or a marriage-like relationship. I feared that as soon as I was ensconced in someone's home — their wife, their partner — I would begin that awful journey towards becoming invisible. If we were tied together with promises of a future, I would be on my way to being forgotten, unheard. It was a precarious space to inhabit: no promises, no future, no joint home, no shared family. Every time I flew south, I didn't know if the older man would want to see me. But each time, he said with impeccable politeness, 'That sounds lovely, why don't you come around.'

On one of these early visits, when I was unsure at the outset whether he would return my desire, we went swimming at the beach. I stripped down to my swimmers, and he to his, and we stood on the edge of the water, exposed, the wind wafting about us. This beach was his home territory, but I'd always been enlivened by the sea. The water was cool and we entered it tentatively, but were soon submerged. I was watching him out of the corner of my eye. This is us, out in the world, I thought, two people, previously lovers, going for a swim. I was filled with a strange mix of apprehension and hope. Would we be lovers again? The water surged around us and I was swept up against him, the skin of my arse brushing his thighs. My whole body erupted in a shiver of goosebumps. Lightly, he laid his hands on my hips under the water, and gently lifted me out of the way. It was a rejection of sorts, but something about it made me smile. He touched me as though he believed I was a grenade that might explode in his hands. As though my desire was so tangible, he had to use all his defusing skills. I glanced at him. Here I am in the bright sunlight, covered in goosebumps, wet and hot inside — what are you going to do? He turned then and began to swim towards the horizon, away from me, and I felt like throwing my head back and laughing. You can run, I thought, but it won't work. It's coming for you, the fragility of desire, of love. How terribly vulnerable it makes us. It wasn't long before he turned around and swam back. I said nothing. He said nothing. We bobbed together in the water. And I knew in that moment that he would press his supple fingers against my skin again soon. He would open me up, touch me with his tongue, find all my secret places and say my name like an incantation, and I knew it from that one brush against him in the waves, skin-to-skin.

'I don't want to presume,' he said that evening, like he had each time.

I climbed onto his lap, shuddery with the knowledge of the pleasure to come. He was older, forlorn. He was no longer the beauty he once had been, but my body swelled with want. It was a mystery, yes? But it was a good one.

~

After the swim, he drove me to his favourite pub. The streets were so quiet the ticking of the indicator seemed loud.

'Goody goody gumdrops,' he said out of nowhere, then flushed a bright pink.

I laughed.

'My god, I haven't said that since I was a child.' He sounded embarrassed.

He was usually so guarded. I loved those moments when something unexpected slipped through.

'Why do you think I like you?' I asked, looking across at him as he drove through the meandering weekend traffic.

'Jessie, I have absolutely no idea.'

I could see this was a problem.

'What's your best guess then?'

Agitated, he swiped a hand through his hair. My question was, apparently, the last question he wanted to answer.

'I don't know. You like that I like dogs?'

I tried not to smile.

'I think we should have a talk about this.'

'Good God, really?'

'Yes,' I reached out to touch his arm, 'because it isn't about the dog.'

On my next visit, a relative was staying with him, so he asked me to meet him in a pub. There was no possibility of sex. We just wanted to lay eyes on each other. We sat out the back in the courtyard, where vines grew thickly over the brick walls. It was dusk and the light was dimming fast. I sensed a strange flickering in the periphery of my vision, but I was so focused on him, I didn't take much notice. After a while, I realised it was mice running all over the vines.

I let out an involuntary squeal, 'Oh, it's alive!'

He laughed, 'I didn't think you would react that way to mice.' He took a sip of his beer. 'You being such a forest-dweller.'

'Well, I love mice.' This time I was embarrassed. 'But they aren't usually running all over the walls in a city pub.'

The mice are out of context, I wanted to say. We are out of context.

We sat close together on a bench on one side of a table, leaning in to one another.

Like a real couple, I thought.

'What do you say to your family when you come down here?' he asked.

'I tell them I have a man I see.' It was true, after all.

He seemed pleased, though I hadn't been sure he would be. Discretion, I'd assumed, was the name of the game.

'I feel, well—' he halted, looking intently at my face '—more than I thought I would,' he continued, flushing. 'More than I expected.'

He looked shamefaced at this confession, at his lack of discipline. It was the first time he'd said anything about his feelings. My body filled with heat. From him — so contained, so reserved

— this felt like a declaration.

I told him that when I was back home, I couldn't stop thinking of his hands.

'You mean touching you?' he asked.

I said, 'Yes, but not necessarily.'

In the dim light, I grasped his hand and put it on my leg. We leaned closer. Two people, in a public space, with feelings and desires.

~

Early on, I told my lover about what I was writing — all my troubles with sex and trauma, attachment and love. About my relationships.

'It's not fiction?' he asked, pressing his fingers down on the tabletop so hard his knuckles turned white.

My memoir, *Staying*, about the suicide of my sister and father in my adolescence, was scheduled for release the following year, but when we'd first met, I'd been a novelist.

I shook my head. 'It's another memoir.'

'Memoir,' he repeated, as if trying to make sense of the word.

I looked down at his fingers, slowly regaining colour.

'Writers—' he paused, and I felt his gaze searching my face '—do what they need to do, I suppose.'

He was magnanimous, but it felt like a kind of surrender.

~

When the older man introduced me to an acquaintance on the street, he always used the word 'friend'. A pause before uttering it, which seemed to enhance its meaning. The acquaintance would glance between us, trying to read the situation. We gave nothing away. The pause hovered, as did the air of uncertainty. It was hard to find a word to fit our relationship. I only ever called him my lover here on the page.

~

Recovering from the tumult, however pleasurable, of my city visits always took some time. After arriving home to the forest, it could take a few days or even weeks to settle back into the rhythm of daily life. Desire was enlivening, but I enjoyed the space between visits to recuperate from it. Each time I left the older man's city, I longed to return. But coming home was always a comfort. It was easier to take risks knowing there was safety at home. Out in the world, I explored those difficult edges — ambivalence, desire, trust, hope, fear — building my tolerance for discomfort and uncertainty, conscious all the while that I had a soft landing. The forest awaited, with all its reciprocated tenderness.

~

When the flood came my family were taken by surprise, even though the weather forecast had been dire for days. A friend messaged the night before: 'I hope you're alright. Stay safe.' And I wrote back, full of nonchalance, 'It floods here all the time. It's nothing new. Don't worry.' But that night it rained like it had never rained before. My room was perched high in the forest canopy, like a bird's nest. I couldn't access it without going out into the weather; when it was raining, I got soaked. That night I'd gone to bed early, before the heavy rain hit. Sometime during the deluge, we lost power. When I woke in the blackness of the night, I knew the rain was different.

In an ordinary flood, the creek swelled to many times its normal size, but the main house was on high land, far out of danger. The little house — the cabin where my smiling boyfriend and I got stuck in the tracksuit pants — was on lower ground, right near the creek. It had always been my mother's retreat from the bustle of the main house, a safe haven at the edges of our property, packed full of memories. In a normal flood, water often came up around the little house, but in the thirty-five years since my father had built it, it had held firm. I knew this new rain meant the little house was in danger, but there was no heading into the night to investigate. The power was gone, and I didn't have a torch in my room. In any case, the rain was so heavy it made vision impossible. The roar of the creek was thunderous, drowning out every other sound. In the darkness, I was both blind and deaf. Incapacitated.

The rest of my family were downstairs, each in their own island bedroom, and I lay awake for the remainder of the night in that frightening pitch-black, hoping they were okay. By first light, the rain had eased. I crept out of bed and raced down the stairs into the main house. I checked my children's bedrooms, sneaking around their sleeping forms. I checked the places in the house that often leaked. There was no substantial damage. I ran across the garden to the path that led down to the little house. From the top of the hill, I saw it was gone. The place where it had once stood, nestled in forest, was bare. Under the cover of night, the raging creek had risen and fallen, broken its banks and claimed our little house. The lack of it, where it had stood for so long, seemed a trick of the eye. I walked to the bottom of the hill and looked downstream: there was the house, crumpled, ripped off its foundations by the force of the water, dumped in a crushed mass.

I ran then, as though in running I could escape what my eyes had seen. When my mother first told me my sister was dead I'd run out into the forest. Help me! I am fleeing to you. Hold me. But when I saw what the water had done to the little house, I ran as fast as I could, straight back to my mother. I stood outside her bedroom door, eyes welling, body shaking. 'Mum,' I cried, 'it's gone. It's all gone!'

She got up slowly, putting on her Japanese dressing gown.

'I knew it would be,' she sighed. 'It has never rained like that before.'

~

We lived on a dead-end road, so if the bridge before our house was damaged by flood, there was no other way out. I drove down to check. The bridge was still standing, but the road on one side had disappeared. We were trapped. I walked across the bridge to where the road had been torn away. An old childhood friend was standing on the other side. She had driven here, so it seemed serendipitous that we should be drawn to opposite sides of the bridge at the same moment. She was with her father.

I called out across the raging creek.

'It's gone!' I was suddenly weeping. 'The little house is gone.'

She looked stricken. Beside her, her father hung his head.

'My mum's house is gone too,' she yelled back. 'It's crazy out here. Everything's destroyed. A woman in Kurrajong died.'

It hit me, like a body blow. My homeland, my homeplace.

'Who was it?' I cried harder.

'We didn't know her. Someone new,' she shouted back. 'It's a horror story.'

'Is your mum alright?' I called out.

My friend nodded. 'She got out before it went.'

Her father, hands on hips, looked up at me and smiled. 'I think I read a story about this sort of thing once,' he called out. 'Flooding, cars washing off bridges.'

It took me a few seconds to realise he was talking about my novel.

'It's all looking very familiar.' Part accusation, part an attempt at cheer.

I giggled, still crying.

'Why don't you write something different next time, Jessie

Cole?' my friend shouted across the water. Since we were kids, she'd always called me by my full name. 'Can I win the lotto?'

'Jess, next time write us something good!' her father echoed. 'None of this flooding shit.'

'Okay, okay,' I concurred, swiping at my tears with the back of my hand, 'I will write us something good.'

~

At home, there was still no electricity, which meant no water. And the landline was dead too. Our forest house was always dark, but without power it was shadowy, desolate. There was no way anyone could get a car across the creek, but on that first day someone in the valley erected a sturdyish footbridge. As soon as it was up, my sons fled the scene, with just the clothes on their backs. I trailed after them, trying to change their minds.

'We can't stay here with no power,' Milla said, walking away from me. Once across the bridge, they planned to hitchhike — destination unspecified.

'But you don't know what's happening out there!' I called to him in panic. 'It could be total chaos.'

The two of them, almost the same size now.

'We're not staying!' they yelled in unison over their shoulders.

'Luca!' I called out, desperate. 'You don't need to go.'

Luca turned around to look at me. 'Mum, we'll be back soon.'

'How will I even know if you're okay?' A wave of powerlessness washed over me.

Please don't leave me, I wanted to shout. How can you leave me?

But they were already gone.

~

Back in the forest, my mother was cataloguing the damage. Whole giant trees knocked over, massive logs strewn everywhere. Metre-high piles of silt and fine leaf matter in strange maze-like walls, impossible to push through. Huge amounts of shattered glass. The occasional stray chair or bedhead littered about from a home similarly stricken upstream. My mother was frantic with grief. She noticed every tree destroyed, every sapling uprooted. She tried to spread out the giant mounds of dumped silt, and pick up the rubbish. She wanted our topsy-turvy world restored and she wanted it right now.

'We have to prop them all up,' she urged me, 'all the trees that are knocked over. If we prop them back up, they'll survive.'

I felt weak at the knees. I wanted out like my children. I could barely lift a twig. My mother's rage grew.

'You're not helping me!' she hissed. 'You need to help me. I can't do it by myself.'

But I couldn't do it at all.

Instead, I took my mobile phone and drove up to the very end of my dead-end road and walked up to the top of the highest hill. Once I'd found a few bars of reception, I messaged my brother and sister. I messaged Lou and Nika and my mother's family, and anyone I thought might be worried about us. 'We are all safe, but the little house is gone,' I said.

I sat there on the hill, my arms wrapped around my knees, weeping, wanting to feel the love of friendship, of family, looking over the vista of my homeplace, listening for the tings of incoming messages.

It mightn't seem much, losing the little house, seeing your forest upended, but it had been my whole world. My safety, my salvation. My parents had planted almost every tree, which had grown around me like a fortress. Keeping me in, keeping the world out. Every year there had been floods, the creeks swelling and the land rearranging. Change was ever-present, but this new rain was beyond what I had known. The forest, my fortress, had been breached.

If the forest isn't solid, are you?

I looked at my phone again and again, waiting to receive some sustenance.

'As long as you are safe. That's all that matters.'

'I'm sorry about the little house. How I loved that place.'

'Darling, how's your mum?'

'Is there anything we can do?'

~

After the flood, my whole body went numb. I stopped registering the heat of our gas oven; my forearms were covered in burns. I also went numb sexually, which wasn't an issue since I had no one nearby to sleep with, but I was surprised that my body could so successfully turn off its nerve endings. When I touched myself, I felt nothing. I wondered how long it might last. Every day, I pinched the skin of my arms, to see if feeling had returned. Every day was the same. I'd experienced numbness in the past, but I hadn't been able to identify the numbness as clearly because I hadn't had so much awareness of feeling. My mother told me that when my sister committed suicide, I'd said, 'I feel like I'm wrapped up in a sleeping bag. It's okay, I'm comfortable. The problem is I just can't move.'

~

When I was a child, flooding would clean out the hidden waterhole at the bottom of the forest, making it deeper, wiping the rocky bottom free of moss and leaves and sticks. After a flood, everything had felt fresh. This new mega-flood, more powerful than we had known, had done the opposite, leaving behind loads of rocks and sticks and silt that filled in our waterhole. The creek had come up so unimaginably high, a giant steel shipping container had crossed a bridge, many kilometres upstream, and arrived at our place. The shipping container, which had held household paraphernalia (an office chair, a bag of sheets, stray photos, miscellaneous plastic bottles filled with unknown substances) had ended up wrapped around one of our trees. It now sat, to my horror, right on top of the boulder where my mother had spent my childhood sunning herself. My mother's rock. It was hard not to see this mass of mangled steel as a desecration.

Our waterhole was not accessible by any vehicle, so there was no way the shipping container could be removed. A few days after the flood, the owner came to look, hopeful that he had not lost the contents. We showed him the contorted steel shell perched on my mother's rock and the small pile of things we had dragged up the forest steps, all of it waterlogged, destroyed.

'The oldies in the home,' he pointed vaguely in the direction of the next big town, 'they didn't know it was flooding till their beds started floating.'

Missives from the outside world.

'It was pitch-black, 'cause no power. The beds drifted around, so they didn't even know where the doors were.'

I remembered that darkness.

'The sound of the rain,' I said, shaking my head, 'was so disorientating.'

'A friend went to help get the oldies out, water up to his thighs, and them all crying about their cats or birds, you know, their critters. 'Cause no one could see a thing.'

We stood together in silence, staring at the pile of his recovered possessions. When he left, he did not take any of these bedraggled objects with him.

—

For the first few days after the flood, my mother battled to prop up every flattened tree, labouring obsessively in our devastated rainforest, trying to clear the debris. My children hadn't returned, and I was overtaken by a heavy malaise that made my body feel like lead. I willed myself to help, even though all the slipping around in the mud felt like a fool's errand. We righted the trees that might be saved. We cleared the walls of silt. We picked our way through the slosh, trying to rescue any stray seedlings. We heaved away the logs we could lift. After all this herculean effort, my mother looked beaten. A rusty, mangled shipping container was covering her rock.

'I don't know if I can live here anymore,' she said.

Sixty-six years old, her back curved, her life's work a shambles. The blow was too much. The destruction too great.

—

I felt stir-crazy at home, trapped in the destroyed forest with no power or water, sifting through the debris. My local writer friend lent me her car. Even though she lived forty minutes' drive away, she left it for me on the other side of my washed-out road, so that I could walk across the rickety footbridge and take a drive into town. Whole sections of my township, and the bigger township nearby, had been submerged. Out on the streets, people were emptying the contents of their homes onto the footpaths. I was gazing into lives far more destroyed than mine. Covered in mud from head to foot, they stared at me as I drove past. I was a voyeur and I was ashamed. In normal times our homes were capsules, all our treasures hidden inside. After the flood, everything was exposed. The trappings of lives spread out on the street, bloated with water and brown with mud. I kept driving, peering out my window with rising horror. All along the roadside lay upturned cars and huge stranded water tanks, capsized caravans and miscellaneous pieces of farm machinery, strewn like an apocalyptic tideline.

~

Ten days after the flood, I flew to the city to visit the older man. The trip had been booked well before the natural disaster, and, in the mess that followed, it seemed too complicated to cancel. On arrival at my brother's house, I started weeping and found to my shock that I couldn't stop.

'I didn't know it would be like this,' I whispered between sobs, 'otherwise I would never have come.'

My brother teared up just watching me. 'Oh, love,' he said.

When I'd texted my family and friends from the highest hill, I hadn't texted the older man. He had never seen my homeplace. I didn't trust him to understand about the loss of the little house. But I'd emailed him once the power came back on, telling him what had happened.

'Oh, I saw that on the telly,' he wrote back. 'I didn't know that it was you.'

He doesn't know where I live, I thought. He doesn't know anything about me. I waited for him to ask if I was still coming to visit, but he didn't. He doesn't care, I thought, wild with sorrow. I am nothing to him.

'Detached,' my brother reflected. 'He sounds very detached.'

In that weepy, broken state I couldn't leave my brother's house. He went to work, so I stayed behind each day with his two cats. They seemed to sense my sadness and snuggled next to me whenever I sat down, one on each side of my body.

I texted the older man to tell him I was in town and he called me straight back.

'I didn't think you would still come,' he said, his voice alarmingly cool.

'I didn't know how to make a decision.' The words spilled out, lines of tears dripping down my face.

'Will you come over?' he asked, as though maybe it would be better if I didn't. 'Come for morning tea on Sunday.'

He wants me to come in the day, so he doesn't have to sleep with me. He's going to break things off! The panic set in and no amount of reality-checking could keep it at bay. Why did I fly my broken self thousands of kilometres through the sky only to be gently rebuffed by someone old enough to be my father? The forest was in ruins, the little house was gone, and here I was in this foreign city attempting to be loved by a man who was detached.

~

I didn't know how I looked when I arrived (pale, puffy, sad), but the man I desired was stand-offish.

He gave me his commiserations. We chatted about the floods. I brimmed with emotion, trying to keep it from spilling over. He did not move to touch me.

He made me a cup of tea and peeled me a mandarin, offering it to me in pieces. The morning slipped by.

'I want to ask you something,' he said, in a lull in our conversation, 'but you don't have to answer it if you don't want to.'

I nodded, wondering what it might be.

'Was it weird to sleep with someone so much older?' he said.

I blushed, against my will. Not expecting that.

'Oh, I've embarrassed you.' He shuffled things about on the kitchen counter. 'Don't answer. It doesn't matter.'

'It was a little bit weird,' I admitted, remembering what his body had looked like over mine that first night. Older than I'd expected. 'But it wasn't weirder than it always is sleeping with someone new.'

He looked at me carefully.

'It is always a bit odd to sleep with someone new,' he conceded. 'But it's doubly hard to get up the courage to sleep with someone twenty years your junior.'

It hadn't struck me before, that he felt vulnerable revealing himself to me. It seemed odd, then and there, that we both felt so confused about the significance of those years between us. That the meaning of the age gap, whatever that meaning was, should continue to be so problematic.

I couldn't read him, as though whatever physical signals I'd once relied on had disappeared. Perhaps the numbness I still felt had cut me off from additional senses? In the void between us, something was rising inside me, some age-old hurt. I was waiting for him to say it, the line that always finishes things. I think we should just be friends. In readiness, my mouth was filling with tears. Whatever was rising started to spill over, words tumbling like small time-bombs off my tongue. I told him how I'd felt in the past about the attentions of old men. How I'd been hit on by some of my father's friends and how much I despised them. I told him that since I'd met him, I'd been looking at old men in a whole new light.

'Maybe old men will be my new thing!' I ended with a kind of wounded defiance. Tear it all down.

'Steady on,' he said with a faint smile, crossing his arms in front of his chest, 'be careful. Not quite "old".'

'Older,' I said. 'Let's stick with that. Older than me.'

He looked uncomfortable.

'I just don't want to have to find someone else to sleep with,' I said quietly, floundering. My lover knew nothing of the somatic obstacles I'd had to overcome to sleep with him. I'd never spoken about my recalcitrant body. 'I don't want to be celibate for the rest of my life.'

He held his arms out, as if he was about to receive me in an embrace, but that space evaporated quickly. Instead, he reached out to place a hand on my shoulder.

'You are a very attractive woman.'

I felt scorned. It was coming, that horrible sentence: but I think we should just be friends.

'It's not that,' I cut in, 'of course it's not that.'

I was stranded there in his kitchen, sinking.

'It's easy to find someone to sleep with,' I said mournfully, as though I'd already lost something precious, 'but I want to sleep with someone nice. It's hard to find someone nice.'

He looked pained. I wanted to retreat, perhaps out the door. I stood up and got myself a glass of water. Sipping it, I stepped back a few paces, wondering how to resurrect myself. Wondering how to leave.

'Do you want to do it now?' he asked, just like that.

I was startled. I'd been so sure he was going to break off with me, my body hadn't even had time to start up its twitching. I pinched my arms, testing if there was any feeling. I couldn't tell.

'Do you?' I stuttered.

He nodded. He wasn't trying to ward me off. My perception had been completely faulty. My disorientation was complete.

⁓

Back in the forest, rain began to have a new meaning for me. In the past, I'd always experienced 'weather events' as exciting. Living in the same house, the same stretch of land all my life, it was often the weather that brought a sense of shifting possibilities. I'd loved the intensity of Northern Rivers rain, pounding on our tin roofs, reminding us that some days there was nothing you could do but watch the creeks rise. I'd loved storms, their electrifying energy. I'd loved how the forest shifted with the wind, how the palm fronds and tree branches bent under the weight of a torrential downpour, how everything adjusted to whatever the skies had to offer.

After the loss of the little house, I loved these things less. When it rained at night, I felt stranded in my canopy room. I lay awake listening to the thrumming, worrying that my children weren't safe below me, worrying that trees would collapse, worrying that if trees collapsed, I would be separated from my family. The forest, which had never seemed menacing to me, began to feel unstable. I was now terrified of high winds. How had I ever slept before? Even on stormless nights, I lay awake listening to the shifting sounds of the surrounding trees, wondering, with heightened hypervigilance, how I would know if one were about to fall. I'd lived my life in blissful ignorance, sleeping through the wildest weather, trusting that my forest would bend and bend and never break, but post-flood I'd awakened to a new world. Trickling creeks could become wild torrents that rose without warning in the night and stole parts of your home. The forest could be upturned. My body, always on high alert, wound even tighter.

~

The little house was where we'd kept all the objects which had broken the banks of our life. Things we loved, or were sentimental about, but did not want to encounter every day. Mugs my dead sister had made in high school, her scrawled name still scratched into the base. Plates that my nanna, a master crafter, had hand-painted. Handmade pottery cups my parents had drunk coffee from when I was a child. An old typewriter, a page of my father's typed words still curled inside. Each of these objects felt imbued with so much meaning, we couldn't have them with us in the main house, but also couldn't quite let them go.

After the flood, we walked as far as we could downstream, but there was nothing much to find, certainly none of the sentimental items. How I craved one of my sister's handmade mugs! To rub my finger along her name. Strangely, a single wine glass survived. Whole, unbroken. For months, I woke in the middle of the night with a new series of lost objects flashing in my mind. I had no conscious memory of the individual items: the plates and notes and knick-knacks, but they were rising in my dreams, the vision of each one perfectly detailed, stored somewhere inside me. There had been so much stashed away in the little house it had been impossible at the time of the flood to remember it all. Too much disappeared at once. Months later, however, my mind was keeping a nightly tally of all the forgotten keepsakes. Each morning I'd wake with a fresh load of loss. Oh, that cup, I'd think. Gone too.

—

After the flood, we could no longer swim in the waterhole. The shape of the creek remained, the curving perimeter as graceful and wide as it had always been, but the pool was now shallow, filled with debris. We could no longer submerge ourselves, let alone frolic. A giant coral tree capsized in the months that followed, its trunk slumped across the middle of the waterhole. In the past, we would have worked to remove a fallen tree, worried it would gather more debris, but there seemed no point post-flood, when there was nowhere left to swim. It was hard to know how to mourn a lost waterhole. When my father had taken his life twenty years earlier, my family had learned to live alongside the memories. Every nook and cranny alive with my father's once-presence. We had learned to cohabitate with the past, but we had done so while held by the forest, the creek system, the waterhole. These places had supported us, when everything else gave way. But now the waterhole was gone too. Another entity to add to the nightly tally of missing cups and beloved knickknacks, steeped in memories and years of pleasure. Uncountable hours of skin-to-skin contact. The most nourishing place I knew, destroyed.

~

A month after the flood, Milla left home. At nineteen he was off to try his luck in a faraway city. With a one-way ticket and a hastily packed bag, my oldest son didn't even need a lift to the airport. So-and-so was taking him, it was all arranged. Milla's departure had been planned, but I was still stunned as I stood in the driveway watching my firstborn fold his big body into that small car.

He beamed through the open car window, 'Bye, Mum!'

Tears gushed down my face as I tried to smile.

'Is your mum okay?' I heard his friend ask.

'Oh, yeah,' my son said, still smiling, 'she always cries.'

I was waiting, he told me later, waiting for you to crack.

'Good luck!' I cried out, not even bothering to wipe away the tears. 'Be safe!'

My son laughed, and I thought of all the bones he'd already broken, the last time I'd rushed him to emergency, his foot shattered from an ill-judged backflip off the back of a truck at schoolies. The nurse took one look at his extensive hospital file and said, 'You've really given your mum a hard time.'

'I love you!' I whispered, watching my son in the departing car. He stretched his long arm out the window and didn't look back.

~

Luca had never liked to sleep alone. Throughout his childhood, I'd lain with him at bedtime, coaxing him into sleep. Some nights, every second of this ritual felt elongated. All the things I'd hoped to do in my blessed after-bedtime beckoned as I tried to breathe through the frustration. Most nights, though, it was soothing. When Luca was still a pre-teen, while I was in the midst of my four-years-of-unrequited-love-hell, I started sleeping in his bed. I told my son it was because the moonlight in my canopy room was so bright I couldn't sleep. I told him I needed to buy blinds. But the truth was I needed to be near him. The truth was the only time I felt safe was when I slept beside him. Luca was overjoyed to have me in his bed. The

Mum-needs-blinds-but-hasn't-yet-bought-them arrangement was his idea of heaven. After a few months, my terror passed. I bought blinds and returned to my own bed.

In the year that Milla left home, his father began to feel unsteady. My ex's life-long equilibrium started to slip: he could no longer be alone. He asked Luca to stay with him a few nights a week. My soothing, glass-half-full child. I wanted to say, you cannot take him from me. I wanted to say, I need him. My son was seventeen and, of course, he got to choose.

Luca said, 'Mum, he needs me.' Simple as that.

Parents aren't supposed to need their children. We are supposed to train them to fly free. We are supposed to self-soothe when they leave. We are supposed to always self-soothe.

~

Lou still had young children, almost all my friends did, and when she called me, she was often interrupted. Children's voices echoed in the background, requesting food, requesting comfort, asking unanswerable questions. Lou listened to me while offering her children bananas, offering them grapes, offering them esoteric, complex explanations. Being on the phone with her was like going back in time, except we had swapped places. I had been her, and she had been me. Our external lives were out of sync, but our inner lives were not. She saved up her thoughts for me, and shared them in snippets between interruptions. A lively, lucid, to-be-continued conversation.

A little while back, I heard a doctor who specialised in palliative care talk about how relatives waiting for the death of their loved one often exclaimed, in a tortured kind of way, 'Oh, how long will this take?' Even when their beloved wasn't suffering. When the doctor told them that he didn't know, that death was unpredictable, they would lament the fact that he couldn't speed up the process, even when there was no apparent pain or struggle. I assumed that if you loved someone you would be thankful for every extra minute you got in their breathing presence, but it seemed the unknowability of when those breaths might end was more painful than the loss itself. At least, with death, the worst had happened. You were no longer stuck in that awful landscape of not-knowing.

I thought about this in reference to my relationship with the older man, who never allowed me to feel a sense of stability. He welcomed me, and he was always kind, but there was never any discussion of a future. But perhaps commitment was simply an attempt to stave off this terror of the unknown? With my particular life experience, I couldn't help but see marriage (or simply commitment) as a kind of cultural delusion that we subscribed to because it gave us a break from the tyranny of daily uncertainty. We all knew uncertainty was the only thing that was certain. You could be hit by a bus tomorrow. It was a cliché, but it was true. How could we make ourselves feel safe in a fundamentally unsafe world?

Make promises we may not be able to keep.

Believe them.

Despite my willingness to participate in this experiment in uncertainty, I relished those moments when my lover's behaviour hinted at coupledom: picking me up from the airport, introducing me to his pub mates, sending me a birthday present, calling me on the weekend, checking in with me after a trying event, planning the next time we might see each other. I longed for those signs that he thought our relationship was ongoing. If too many of them occurred in a row, I would find myself slipping into a complacent acceptance that we were, indeed, a couple.

~

Last visit we did all the usual activities — restaurant, movies, evening stroll around the neighbourhood, sex. Afterwards, he got up, put on his pants, and said, 'You know, I like all the other things around sex too. Spending time together, doing things. All that stuff you do before and after. For me, they're part of what makes it nice.'

His comment was bewildering. I was still naked, post-orgasm-languid, heartbeat fluttering pleasantly in my chest. What was I being accused of? Only liking sex? I wanted to laugh, but my lover seemed serious. Possibly peeved. I thought I was following parameters he'd set, but maybe he thought he was following mine?

I sat up, shrugging, the way I knew my mother would have

when my father got blustery.

'I like them both,' I said. 'I like them both equally.'

~

About eighteen months into our relationship, when I told the man I desired I was planning to visit, he invited me to stay at his house. To stay for the whole week. It seemed we were shifting to a more settled connection. I was relieved — my longing for a sense of ongoingness assuaged. It also gave my beleaguered nervous system a break. I still arrived trembly and swollen-tongued, but after a day or so those symptoms usually disappeared.

Being a guest in my lover's house was a pleasure. He took hospitality seriously. I always arrived before he was home from work; he would leave the key out for me. On the end of the bed, there'd be a selection of books he'd chosen, titles he thought I might enjoy. I didn't eat wheat, and in the breadbox there'd be fresh specialty bread. If I'd commented the visit before about a particular food I liked, he'd have stocked up on it. In my life in the forest, I was always tending to others, but when I visited my lover, he tended to me. He fussed around with my towel, hanging it out in the sun, making sure it was always warm and dry.

~

The longer visits developed a distinct pattern. We would spend a few days together in easy harmony and then, all of a sudden, my

118

lover would turn icy. He did not say anything, but I felt he was no longer receptive to me. Yes, it was simply *a feeling*. It was as if he had erected a forcefield around him, and I could not break through. I would, of course, panic, but I'd been with him long enough to know, when he was in this state, that any bids for reassurance would be deflected, which only exacerbated my dread. When he became icy, I was convinced that he actively disliked me, found me intolerable. I should leave, I'd think, but where would I go? Should I just walk out? When this happened, I quickly became overwrought, terrified. I knew these feelings were excessive so I kept them to myself. Sometimes his forcefield would stay up for a whole day! I was lost. I couldn't go on. And then, with as little warning as when he disappeared into the unreceptive zone, he would re-emerge, and it was as if it never happened. He was cheerful again, seemingly unaware of his prior state. My nerves were shot. I'd been through the wringer. I was ecstatic to be allowed close again, but also worn and weary from the strain of waiting. This strange cycle of connection and withdrawal was completely unacknowledged between us.

~

Since my father's death, my most serious romantic relationships had all involved a feeling of impending doom. A sense that equilibrium was an impossible fantasy. Everything felt fraught. The smallest mishaps caused undue stress. I believed the relationship was always on the rocks. One false move and it would disintegrate. All the ways I was unlovable would be discovered. I would be left. I was constantly on guard for the slightest rejections, and this vigilance did not allow much space for the other person to experience slips in attentiveness. Small moments of carelessness — things I didn't focus on in my female friendships — quickly became magnified in my romantic relationships. But if everything felt like a red flag, how could I distinguish which red flags mattered? My sensitivity was sky-high. In under three seconds, I could escalate from a minor threat to the wildest sense of loss. Could my father's final act have had so much power?

—

To counter my obsessive tracking of red flags, I reminded myself of the ways my lover and I were close. The older man didn't talk easily about himself, not the way I did. But I'd spent a lifetime with people less directly expressive than me — my mother, my brother — and I'd learned how to leave space, silence. To ask questions at the right times, to wait patiently for the answers. I wanted to know my lover — his past, his thoughts, his feelings — so I watched and I asked and I waited. Although sometimes cagey, mostly he would speak.

—

One day, lying in bed, my lover said, out of the blue —
   'Sometimes I go quiet.'
   I lay still, stunned by his revelation. He knows.

'Yes, sometimes I feel that,' I said tentatively.

He didn't look at me.

'What's happening inside your mind when you go quiet?' I asked. 'Is it quiet inside your mind?'

'Oh, no, it's never quiet in there.' He was still looking away.

'So, what is it?'

'I just don't feel like talking.'

'Maybe it's an introvert thing and you need a bit of time to recharge?'

I felt him relax, his body loosening beside me.

'Yes, I've never thought about that.' He was radiating relief. 'Maybe that's all it is.'

He goes quiet.

I wondered how many women in his life had panicked as I had. How many women had dissolved into needy tears? It turned out my lover simply reached a saturation point, and when he reached it, he went quiet. His withdrawal, so painful to experience, so seemingly personal, was just his need clashing with my need. In healthy relationships, were the negotiations over whose need was met simply less fraught? He turned towards me and pulled me into a hug. I lay in his embrace, holding tight to that warm feeling.

This was it, my need being met.

~

At some early point in my visit, the older man often said —

'Only if you want to. I mean, I could set up the spare room.'

Despite my ongoing, obvious desire to sleep with him, he knew every encounter in the past stood for nothing in the here and now. He never wanted to presume. Which meant I was almost always the one to initiate sex. In the beginning, I found his stand-offishness terrifying. That first time, he'd been so indecisive I'd assumed myself rejected for almost an hour. Did I have to sit in that intensely uncomfortable space every time I saw him? Did I have to risk my dignity, my self-esteem, my nervous system every single visit? But as time passed, I became braver, or more comfortable with that particular discomfort, or perhaps more trusting of his kindness. If my desire, in any given moment, was not reciprocated, my dignity wasn't at stake. My worthiness was not so attached to his response to me. I could be, in that moment of rejection, undesired, but still acceptable to myself. It was a revelation. And that, in itself, was a revelation.

~

As an adult, I felt giddy relief when a sexual partner made a bid for sex and backed off at the first sign of my non-interest. I was filled with joy and gratitude. The man simply understood that I didn't owe him sex, but for me it felt like a miracle. An extreme reaction, I admit.

After my first relationship ended, I feared having to re-enter a state of relentless pursuit, which I'd believed, as a young person, all heterosexual relationships entailed. Back then, I hadn't been able to envisage an interaction in which I had autonomy, in which my right to be not interested in an erect penis was respected.

~

'Has he come to visit you?' When discussing my relationship with the older man, I was often asked this question. Quickly followed by, 'Because he can't really know you till he sees you in your home.'

I wondered if this was true for everyone, or only true for forest-dwelling me.

Every now and then, when I knew my mother would be away, I asked my lover to visit me. Each time, he promptly rejected the idea and changed the subject. I assumed that a visit was too much of a commitment for him, but I shrugged off each small rejection. Did he need to see me in my homeplace to truly know me? Was I not myself when I stayed at his house?

My mother was away for a month or so, and I asked my lover to visit again, and this time, with almost no prevaricating, he said, 'Yes, that sounds very nice,' and booked a flight.

He was quiet on arrival, taking it in, all the separate rooms, divided by the forest. Inside was large and spacious and dark and cool. Outside was luminous green, otherworldly. I hadn't even tried to warn him.

'This is really something else,' he said finally, one eyebrow raised.

I nodded. Yes, yes it is.

I didn't know if I seemed different to him in my own home, but my lover seemed different to me. Looser, energised, enlivened. On the last day he climbed onto my children's old trampoline and jumped higher and higher, like a child. I watched him from the corner of my eye as I hung out the washing. He was losing years, bouncing on that trampoline. He looked so joyous, I wondered why it had taken him so long to come.

~

My memoir, *Staying*, was scheduled for release. Back in his city, my lover called. Somewhere in the conversation he mentioned that he would soon read it. I was filled with instant dread. He knew the basics of my story — the suicides of my sister and father — I'd told him on the day we met, but we rarely talked about it. In my mind, it had seemed a far-off possibility that my lover would one day read the words I'd struggled so hard and so long to bring into the light.

Suddenly, I was fighting tears.

'But why will you read it?' I asked.

'It will be in bookshops. Of course I'll read it,' he said gently.

I was mute with terror. How could I have not realised this sooner?

'Jessie?' his voice was soft, warm. I was trying to let it guide me.

'It's just, I don't want you to see me differently.'

I could feel the tears dripping down my cheeks, pooling in

the corners of my mouth.

'Oh,' he said. I heard his surprise.

'I hadn't imagined you would read it.'

I didn't want my book to bust open the delicate trust we had built. But I was also afraid that, if he knew, in the detail the book revealed, what I'd been through, he would turn away from me. My past would act as a repellent. I was bracing for the worst.

'Everyone will read it,' he murmured. 'It will be read.'

Everyone who wants to will read it, I thought. Not *everyone*.

'Okay,' I said. It was out of my hands.

'Okay,' he echoed softly.

—

As he read my memoir, he sent me updates. The page he was on, what he was thinking. Brief missives. It turned out we would do this together. His kindness made my chest hurt.

On page eighty-one, 'I'm crying now.'

And then nothing.

I knew the wide arc he was moving through, the wide arc of pain and loss and madness and grief. There was nothing to say to make it right. I waited for him to resurface. Despite my earlier terror, I was strangely calm. We were travelling on the same seas, just years apart. He would know me; I would be known. When he finished the book, we would be at the same destination.

The present. The here and now.

He sent a message. He had arrived.

He didn't say it, but I knew it anyway. All would be well.

—

The next time I flew to his city we walked around his neighbourhood. We never usually went to the pub at the end of his street, but it was a cool day and there was an inviting sunny patch on the street outside. We decided to stop and get a drink. We sat side by side on a bench in the sun. Up close, we stared at each other's faces.

'You have a little vein here,' he said, his fingertip brushing just below my eye. 'It's new.'

I smiled. 'It's always there,' I said. 'You've just never been this close to me in bright light.'

He flushed, and smiled, and suddenly it was all there in his face: he was full of feeling.

He loves me, I thought. He mightn't know it yet, but he does. The pleasure of the revelation hit me full in the belly.

'Yes, we are usually in the dark,' he said with a chuckle. 'That's true.'

I grazed his shoulder with my cheek, the briefest touch.

stormy seas

On one of my longer visits, my lover and I went for a walk around his local park, in amongst the wintry trees. I liked to look at him out in the world. His upright posture beneath clothes, his beautiful hands hidden in his pockets. He wasn't watching me, but looking out for dogs. Since the loss of his beloved old dog, he watched other people's dogs with a barely concealed longing. There were a few kids among the dogs, and my lover and I got into a hypothetical discussion about what kind of future scenario would mean we each might contemplate having more children. He said that if he was 'sufficiently in love' he might consider it. There were a few things about his use of that phrase that got under my skin. Firstly, that being 'in love' should have any relevance to the raising of children. Secondly, by what criteria he would judge if his love was 'sufficient'. Thirdly, and most disturbingly, there was something about the way he uttered the phrase that made me fairly sure that he thought he was *not* sufficiently in love with me.

I didn't want to have any more children. Nevertheless, my

woundedness surfaced in one huge swell. There was a tidal wave in my heart. We had never spoken about love or being in love and the sudden introduction of the topic into our conversation left me reeling. Was this the moment when an emotionally sturdy person would be brave enough to ask, 'Do you love me?' Or, perhaps more tentatively, 'Do you think you might one day love me?' It was not the kind of question I would ever ask. I imagine my face was stony. I began to read all sorts of things into our conversation — that he assumed I understood he was not sufficiently in love with me, that it was clear between us love was not a thing we were doing, that he expected to find someone he could be sufficiently in love with in the near future, that even though he would dedicate time to me, and fuck me as requested, it was not sufficient, that I was not sufficient, that I would never be sufficient, that he would never love me. It was a swift spiral. All of a sudden, I was in ruins.

As I walked quietly beside him in the park, I expressed none of this turmoil. I had never asked him to love me, or admitted, even to myself, that I might require this from him. Did I require it? How well did I understand love in a sexual-relationship context? I loved my friends and family with an ease and simplicity that I had no trouble either expressing or understanding, but this kind of love felt different.

For days after our conversation I couldn't stop ruminating on his phrase 'sufficiently in love'. Maybe I imagined it, but my lover seemed to spit it out, with some disdain. Did he feel the same kind of ambivalence I did for the experience of being in love? Or was my own ambivalence colouring my perception of his disdain? It was a lost moment. I could never go back to the conversation and ask him to explain. He probably wouldn't even remember saying those words. They probably meant nothing to him. They were probably noteworthy only in that they showed up a discrepancy between how we both perceived what was necessary for child-rearing. It was a hypothetical conversation, for god's sake! Were hypothetical conversations always the most dangerous? All that secret longing on display.

~

Although my other oddball physical tics had settled, my vagina still gave me trouble. What it did, and what it had done for some years, was become inflamed at the very prospect of sex. When I say inflamed, I do not mean in a good way, but rather: irritated, sometimes even sore. There are innumerable possible explanations for vaginal inflammation, and I'd been tested for every one it was possible to test for. I never got a clear answer. Frustrated, I visited a new gynaecologist a couple of hours away, someone who had come highly recommended. I sat in a chair with stirrups and she took photographs of my vulva, which she then projected onto a big screen. I committed to the medicine she prescribed, and it quickly brought down the inflammation, but it didn't prevent the pre-sexual-contact flare-ups that I had to treat before a visit to my lover. If I had a highly sensitive vagina, it made sense that the tissue might be disturbed by sex, however — a preparation-for-sex response?

'Inflammation is just your body working to heal,' my gynae-cologist said at my next appointment. 'If, historically, your body has had to heal after sex, your body has learnt to prepare for this possibility.'

'It's jumping the gun?'

'Yes, so to speak.'

'Why does my body think sex will require healing?'

She looked out the window. Did she think I'd been raped or sexually abused? Had my body told her that? I felt this assumption sitting between us. Intense, unspoken.

'The more positive sexual experiences you have,' she said, 'the more your body will unlearn this behaviour.'

'Okay,' I replied, trying to make sense of her subtext, 'but it is hard to have positive sexual experiences if I'm always anxious about my vagina being inflamed.'

I wished she'd speak to me specifically about what qualified as sexual trauma. I thought about what my body had been through. Was any of it enough?

'Do you have any tips on interrupting this cycle?' I asked.

She shuffled her papers, impatient. This conversation was not what she was paid for.

'It will get better, your body will learn.'

It wasn't a satisfying answer, but it was all I got.

On the way home in the car I remembered the old hippie idea of 'white-lighting'. Visualising yourself, or someone else, in a protective white light. I tried to visualise the white light beaming vibrantly around my vagina. This is what I've come to, I thought. Just the fucking white light.

~

I once read a Goodreads review of my first novel that stated, 'this author clearly has daddy-issues'. Never have I felt so awfully, terrifyingly seen. I wondered how this anonymous person might feel about deriding my work if they knew just how true the statement was. My father committed suicide when I was eighteen, a very young adult. He left me reeling. He left me distraught. But mostly he just left me. That my 'daddy-issues' would be apparent in my fiction was no surprise to me. That I might be seen as failing in my writing because that part of my life swam to the surface in my fiction was more confusing. It was startling how often the wounds we carried were repackaged like failures and thrown back in our faces. My father's final choice affected me in ways too various to catalogue, but somehow, in order to retain a sense of dignity, I was supposed to attempt to hide the damage from view. Even in my art, according to that scornful reviewer. It was a double weight to carry: the woundedness itself, and the need to hide the woundedness.

~

Freud's compulsion-repetition theory — that through subconscious mechanisms, we replay past traumatic events in order to try to resolve them — is relatively popular in alternative rural Australia. In my homeland, Freud's theory is often conflated with the belief that 'the universe' is teaching you something, so that every setback can be read as a lesson you, and specifically you, need to experience in order to reach enlightenment, or happiness, or inner peace. It's like a form of semi-religious faith, not far removed from the idea that God has a plan for you.

As comforting as this may be, I abhorred the narcissism inherent in the belief that everything happens for a reason — that 'the universe' conspires to teach you things in order for you to grow, including such horrific experiences as losing a loved one to suicide or a baby to cot death, or being abused as a child. While I understood the desire to find meaning in chaos, I was sceptical about these beliefs and theories. A friend told me she'd come to understand that she chose men who failed her — even set them up to fail — in order to live in the wounded state with which she was so familiar. In this theory, we chose the familiar over something fundamentally healthier, in order to preserve the status quo, which, even though unsafe, *felt* safer. After falling for ambivalent men over and over, I understood why the theory might hold water. But in my case, my father was (relatively) loving and supportive until the sudden suicide of my sister, when he slowly lost his mind. His eventual suicide wounded me like nothing ever had, but his actions didn't follow on from years of mistreatment by him. On the contrary, my earliest and most formative decade was spent basking in his affection. To imagine that I was replaying my father's abandonment seemed overly simplistic, especially since I hadn't yet had a lover leave me out of the blue. And it didn't quite ring true that the 'woundedness' my father inflicted on me would feel more familiar than the many years of his love.

What if, instead, it was the promise of my father's kind of love — open, easy, receptive, trust-engendering, verbalised, unconditional — that was undermined by his suicide? What if I chose (or was attracted to) ambivalent men precisely because they didn't make overt promises? Ambivalent men were uncertain, undecided. What if ambivalence felt safer to me because my father chose to leave me (radically) after years of professing unconditional and everlasting love? What if I was not replaying an abandonment again and again, but was trying to live wisely in a world full of uncertainties?

My father's receptiveness was what I missed mostly, and struggled to find, in the dance of intimacy in my relationships with men since his death. I liked to feel that I would be welcomed if I needed a hug — maybe a lot of them — but the men I'd been attracted to seemed to have a limit to the amount of affection they could tolerate giving or receiving. Did I need to be a little rebuffed to be aroused? And if so, was this a sexual (life) malfunction?

My older man fitted the bill of needing more personal space than I would have preferred. Sometimes he was receptive to a hug, at other times he wasn't; it was hard to tell when was the right time. If left to my own devices, I might try to sit all over him like I used to with my dad, which — yes — was a disturbing image. I didn't do it, as I knew he wouldn't like it. But I probably got one-sixth of the hugs I wanted from him, perhaps fewer. Even though I needed hugs, being rejected was more painful than the need, so most of the time I didn't try to meet the need. It was easier to initiate sex than to initiate hugging, which put me in the awkward position of seeming like a nymphomaniac, when actually what I most desired from him was affection. How many women (and men?) got caught in this trap? I was willing to bet it was a few.

~

Two years into our relationship, the man I desired told me my breasts were 'magnificent'. It was the only time he commented on my body, except for the first night he saw me naked, when he looked down at the wild, criss-crossing stretchmarks and scars on my belly, and asked simply, 'What happened here?' It had troubled me that a man his age, with (presumably) a swag of lovers behind him, would have to ask that question. Was it one more hint at just how different my body might be? I didn't want to interrupt the moment with the sad tale of my birthing experiences, so I smiled and said, 'I just had big babies.' A half-truth, but it went some way to explaining it.

I have big breasts, big in the way that some men were

purported to like. But, in my experience, their size was generally off-putting. It was as though my big breasts set me up as more sexually 'on', or more sensual, than I was. As though I was ensuring that men were already on the back foot, as though — through my breasts — I was engaging in a form of aggressive visual signalling. I couldn't do anything about the cultural messaging my body displayed, apart from wearing clothes that minimised my cleavage or hid these 'signallers' to the best of my ability. I once had a friend report that a mate of hers had said, 'What's the go with Jess's breasts?' (Irritated sigh.) 'Does she control the tides with them?' I'd laughed on hearing about his consternation, but it confirmed my hunch that some men found my breasts disconcerting.

I didn't think of my breasts as magnificent. I wished that I did. My lover's compliment gave me an unexpected thrill. He had never admitted to finding me beautiful (apart from the lone 'attractive woman' statement, when I'd thought he'd been trying to end things). Was that strange? We often assume desire is predicated on beauty — it's what our culture consistently tells us — but perhaps it simply isn't? I found my lover beautiful, though I saw him as he was — thinning hair, lined face, narrow old-man shoulders. But his beauty was not necessarily why I desired him. His hands were slender and graceful, the skin very smooth. The way he moved his hands in everyday life — readying a teapot, making toast — alerted me in some way to his sensuality. When I watched his hands it made me wet. Not instantaneously. My arousal built throughout the day. Part of my fixation with his hands must have been because I'd experienced his skilful use of them, so it was easy to imagine them touching me the way I liked. Perhaps his hands acted as a signifier, the way my breasts seemed to — a signifier of sexual skilfulness rather than avail-ability or receptivity.

When I was back in the forest, away from my lover, I would imagine his hands. Sometimes I thought of them on my skin, but often I simply thought of the way he used them as he went about his daily tasks, and this was enough to kindle my arousal. But I didn't know the power his hands had when I first met him, and yet my desire for him was still there. Did I somehow intuit it? Was it encoded in his body language? Was my animal body simply responding to his? And if so, was it safe to assume that it wasn't *only* his beauty?

~

Our culture is permeated with the notion that beauty and desire are inextricably linked. But desire doesn't always obey the dictates of cultural sanctions. Desire is an unruly beast. How much does power come into play? There are, of course, unending examples of the powerful forcing their desires on the unwilling. Situations where no mutuality or reciprocity of desire or arousal exists. But can someone's perceived power or social status sometimes create a magnetic attraction? Does the power (celebrity?) of pop stars or footballers, for example, increase the likelihood that a person might become aroused in their presence? Or is that kind of sex about other desires altogether? Sleeping with people just to feel a sense of conquest. As a form of personal empowerment. How do these motives correlate with actual arousal? Was my lover's position as a white older man in a culture where white older men traditionally held most of the power something that did it for me? Was it even possible to separate him — and what I desired about him — from his privilege? Could we ever just be two bodies fucking in the dark?

~

My lover called me on a Friday night, when I was staying at Nika's.

'Guess what happened?' he said, with some agitation. 'You are going to love this!'

He never began conversations this way. It was impossible for me to guess.

'I was at the pub, and I bumped into that woman we had a chat with at the restaurant when you were here last.'

I vaguely remembered. Lots of makeup, blonde hair.

'She asked me where my daughter was tonight.' He said it quickly, as if he was getting it off his chest.

'What?' I was having trouble orientating myself, still waiting for the thing I was going to love. 'But you don't have a daughter.'

'She thought you were my daughter.' He sounded mortified.

'Oh,' I said, as it fell into place. 'Really?'

I didn't love that news.

I remembered us, on the night in question. The picture we made. It was possible we looked like father and daughter, but it was an irksome image. Because we were lovers, I always assumed we looked like lovers. Sometimes when we passed a shop window, I'd see the older man wince at the sight of us together, caught for a moment in the glass. 'We don't match,' he'd said once, perturbed. I saw it, this disparity, but perhaps, living in the forest, I was less attuned to the reflected view.

'I thought you would enjoy that.' He sounded confused. Wasn't it an undeniable fact that all women wished to be seen as young?

I didn't know how to respond. I didn't enjoy things that caused him discomfort.

'She can't have been looking too closely,' I said finally, willing the conversation to turn.

That's it, I thought, after he'd hung up. I'm growing my hair out.

I'd been going grey since my late twenties, but dying my hair. Once you start, it's hard to stop. Once the bulk of your hair has turned grey, and is continuously dyed, it's no longer a question of whether you can live with a few shimmering strands. The issue becomes how to transition to a completely new you. I'd been considering it for a while, but my lover's phone call was the decider. My father had been grey by the time I was born, my mother, always light-haired, was a beautiful silver-blonde, and even my brother, two years younger, was greying up nicely. I was ready to join my silver-haired clan.

The last time I'd seen him, my lover surprised me with the proclamation, out of nowhere, that, in fact, we had only been together five times.

It's been over two years! I wanted to cry.

I steadied myself instead and counted up how many times my lover and I had been together in the same place and came to the number twelve — it had been every two months or so.

'It's been more than twice that,' I said as calmly as I could.

Did he not remember? Was I the most trifling thing? So easily forgettable? My body reacted with alarm — trembling, constricted heart — but some deeper part of me knew he was afraid. As afraid as I was.

'But all those earlier times, they don't really count,' he said.

It had all counted to me, but I accepted he saw it differently. My visits counted now, I noted. These five longer stays. But what did they count towards?

How long could we exist in a limbo state? Was there a limit? We were at the edges of it, I was sure. By reducing our encounters to five, my lover was signalling to me that I had misread the earlier signs of his care as signals of commitment, that — too early on — I'd felt a sense of security in something that wasn't really secure. I absorbed this message, but I was getting better at not panicking. I no longer, so quickly, went into emotional freefall. He is kind, I'd think, but he is scared. He will do his best, I'd think, but it may not be enough. He will not turn me away, even if he no longer wishes to have sex. We are friends, I'd reassure myself. What we do or don't do with our bodies, in unison, is not the most important part.

What was the most important part, then? The here and now, of course. I know those words hold within them the horrific echo of a thousand yogi-wannabes. Trite wisdom, so popular in my homeland. But whenever my lover called me, I fought the need to read it as a signal there was something ongoing and reliable between us. I tried to see the phone call as something more simple: we are speaking now. I am hearing the pleasurable intonations of his voice. Sometimes he would laugh in that gurgly, sensuous way. Oh, how I loved the sound!

'Take care,' he'd say at the end. The closest I'd ever get to a declaration.

~

During my next visit to my lover, I met up with a new writing friend in the city for lunch. We were in a crowded cafe, but straight up she asked me what I was writing, and I told her it was a memoir about my struggles with my recalcitrant body and sex.

She looked at me with such understanding, I didn't even feel ashamed.

'When it comes to sex,' she said, 'there are all those prescribed ways to do it.'

I nodded, desperate to know where she was going with that thought.

'A whole host of culturally agreed upon positions and behaviours.'

The cafe was cacophonous, but I was so focused on her words the clattering sounds receded.

'But, Jess, your sexuality seems spread out, your whole being in a sensuous relationship with your world. It's not locked in that one space and time! Maybe this makes it more confusing for you, and your body, when you're locked into those prescribed physical positions with somebody else?'

I looked at my new friend, aghast. She had never experienced me as a sexual being — how could she assume these things? Sitting opposite her, I was suddenly intensely self-conscious. What was she seeing? Did everyone see it? My face was now very hot. Was that how my lover saw me? I tried to think back on how I behaved in my lover's house. It was small and very tidy, and I was constantly disrupting that tidiness with my unruliness. I tried hard not to make ripples of disturbance in his environment, but I often failed. Was my sensuousness 'spreading out', as she said, around me all the time? Did my habits, learned in the forest, make me a strange creature to my lover?

I'd already observed that he had a generous way of down-playing my deficiencies. He was much more knowledgeable than me in many areas, especially art and culture, but if we happened into a conversation where my lack of expertise was apparent, he would deftly change course. I didn't mind acknowledging my ignorance, but he tried to help me avoid doing that. It was touching to witness. The very opposite of mansplaining. He seemed to do it naturally. Did that mean he avoided letting me know when I had revealed other, less appealing parts of who I was? He was excruciatingly observant, so I presumed this was the case.

—

Months later, it struck me that my writer friend's left-of-field observations about my sexuality might have been based on impressions she'd gleaned from reading my books. Both my novels were exercises in embodiment of another person, in escape from self, in exploring sexuality in a safe (fantasy) place. I wondered if my body of work was building a kind of alter-ego self, the person I was in fiction, quite different from the person I felt myself to be in my life. It was impossible, of course, to view myself from outside my own body. My eyes always sat inside my own skull. Mirrors and photographs and films captured me from an outside view, but it was only a reflection of the physical body, and only the fragments that could be seen. The writing-self involved the interior, things not on display. And things I didn't necessarily know about myself might be seen by others in my writing. My lover had read my books. I wondered if they coloured how he saw me.

Back home, I wanted to send him a selfie of me in my bed, reading. I wanted to caption it *all this could be yours*, hoping he'd read the slightly ironic but still hopeful undertone. But when I stared at the photograph all I saw was how messy my surroundings would look to him. *Enter my chaos, I dare you* was how I assumed he might read it. And I wasn't hopeful that, on receiving the photograph, he would want to try.

~

My lover was a discerning gift-chooser. The gifts he sent me were always aligned with my interests and aesthetically appealing. Mostly books, an occasional item of clothing. On my visits to his city, I sometimes accompanied him while he shopped for someone else and observed his careful decision-making. In contrast, I was an ad hoc gift-giver. My family culture prioritised the handmade creation of a gift, or its uniqueness. I sent my lover occasional presents in the post — a wonky mug I made in pottery class, a banksia seedpod, polished and hollowed out to create an oil diffuser. This is perfect, I'd think, impulsively, wrapping it up and sending it before I could change my mind.

When he received these gifts, he would call me.

'Thank you,' he'd say, 'it's lovely.' A bemused pause. 'Just, what is it?'

~

Once or twice a year my lover, an immigrant, flew home for a longish stretch. It was never more than two months, about the same time we usually spent apart, but when he was out of the country, I missed him dreadfully. Often on these holidays his communication would drop off. I tried not to express my anxiety, as I wanted him to feel relaxed at home. But I would worry, unaccountably, that he was dead. Who would tell me? Did anyone in his life have my contact details? I doubted it. Who could I call to check that he wasn't dead? Did I have the contact details of anyone in his life? Of course, I could have just called *him*, but once I was in that thought-looping state, contacting him was out of the question.

~

In an attempt to understand love, I began reading about attachment theory. I read a 500-page scholarly book. The theory was based on the idea that babies became 'secure' or 'insecure' attachers according to how attuned their primary caregiver is to their needs. Insecure attachers were generally either anxious, having received inconsistent care, or avoidant, having been chronically rejected, separated, or 'mis-attuned'. Sometimes this mis-attunement was caused by cultural beliefs about childrearing: ideas about teaching a baby or child resilience through not meeting its needs, for example.

I saw why it was an area of scholarship that had been hugely contested, especially when it came to measuring a mother's (yes, usually a mother's) effect on her baby. Measuring the degree of connection. Measuring the effects of love or a lack of it. Measuring the degree of brokenness of the mother–child bond, and what the outcome of this less-than-ideal mothering might be. Studies showed that insecurely attached children had adverse outcomes in a whole range of areas, but most spectacularly (for my interests, at least) in their ability to form healthy relationships. There was no consensus on how fixed the attachment styles were, though there was some evidence that they could be altered over time by more attuned care. Or, similarly, that a secure attachment style might be upended by a sudden separation or, in the worst case, by death. My father died when I was on the brink of adulthood, and he died by suicide, which — according to the attachment data — had a particularly strong impact. Was I still young enough, at that age, to have my attachment style overturned? From secure to insecure? Maybe it could happen at any age? Maybe it could be an after-effect of many types of betrayal? There didn't seem to be much data on this.

~

I told my lover over the phone that I'd been reading a 500-page book on attachment theory. But I was really trying to tell him something else entirely.

He seemed to understand that my words held extra meaning.

'Why are you reading that?' he asked, on cue.

'I'm … interested.'

Even though he had asked the right question, I was floundering.

I stuttered through the basics of attachment theory, sensing my lover's boredom. I suspected my lover was an avoidant attacher, but I didn't mention that. He was mildly dismissive of the theory of attachment, as though I'd been rambling on about numerology, or something equally despised by the rational-minded. But the data showed that avoidant attachers were known to dismiss the importance of attachment, and attachment theory. I didn't tell my lover that either.

Anxious attachers in adulthood were obsessed with their attachment relationships and I had a hunch that only an obsessive would read a 500-page scholarly book on a subject they were not receiving a qualification for. As likely as my detached lover using dismissive language when the subject was raised. Anxious attachers were the most embarrassing: they sent 200 text messages when one of theirs was ignored; they spiralled out of control at the first sign of abandonment; they read rejection in everything and couldn't suppress their terror. But the worst part about anxious attachers was their tendency to be attracted to avoidant attachers who continuously pressed their abandonment buttons.

At what point did researchers or psychologists define attachment issues as a 'disorder', I wondered. Did I have this disorder? I immediately imagined my lover's disdain at my stewing over a topic he considered unscientific and irrelevant. Mortification flooded in. It was always so uncool to be the one who cared more, and I was the uncoolest of them all.

~

Reading about attachment theory, it was hard not to think of the ways my mothering might have affected my own children. I knew I hadn't neglected my sons, but perhaps I'd gone the other way and been smothering.

During Milla's delinquent years, he proclaimed with lightning insight, 'You know what your problem is? You love me too much.' At the time I was aghast. Was it possible to love a child too much? But attunement was at the core of secure attachment, not the grandiosity of love. It's possible that my love for Milla had sometimes overwhelmed my ability to intuit his needs, especially for independence.

~

Milla returned from his city jaunt, some of the wind taken out of his sails, the shattered bones in his foot still giving him trouble. Both my sons lived at home again — going off to work — but now they had girlfriends. How these girls came to live in the forest, and how our home became their chosen home, was different for each girl. One arrived with all her things, whereas the other moved in incrementally, and I was yet to see one item of clothing or possession left behind in her comings and goings. I didn't interfere or comment. What wisdom did I have to share? I was certainly no authority on relationships. My transition from mother to friend or housemate had been a long time coming, and it was difficult for me to step back and allow my sons to make their own mistakes, but I enjoyed the vibrancy of their grown-up presence in the house. My mother had never pushed me from the nest and I was loath to force my children to fly. I hoped that when they were ready, I would be ready too.

Milla was still boisterous. He came into the main area of the house for chats, and he cooked for us most nights. His girlfriend was forced by this behaviour to be relatively sociable. Luca still liked to lie low. He and his girlfriend rarely emerged from their room, where they watched endless movies, and seemed to laugh and chatter their home days away. If I wanted to ask Luca a question, I had to knock on the door and step inside to where he and his girlfriend were always curled up on his bed. It felt strange witnessing my sons' blossoming sexual lives, when they had witnessed so little of mine. As a single mother, I'd worked hard to shield my children from the possible weirdness or discomfort of watching me with lovers who weren't their father, but here I was surrounded by my sons' easy intimacy, knocking on their bedroom doors, not knowing what I might find.

~

When Milla moved back with his girlfriend, they brought a kitten with them — not desexed. Pure white, and pretty as fine porcelain. Very soon she was on heat: behaving aggressively, forever fighting to be let outside, slipping out during the slightest lapse in our concentration. Once out, she didn't come home at night. Cats come on heat in cycles. After the period ends, they go back to the quiet, sleepy creatures they usually are: rational, no longer pawing at the doors, easily placated with a few strokes, curling up in your lap. I was startled by the strength and persistence of our kitten's desire to mate. How easy it was for us to forget we were animals.

~

Before we desexed her, the kitten had kittens, a young mum, like I'd been. Milla and his girlfriend occupied the garage bedroom, a separate dwelling — we were growing satellite families in the forest, like spores. Cats are predators, we all know that, but in our forest they are also prey. The carpet snakes hunted them, especially the kittens. The snakes hung down from the trees, waiting for the babies to try to slip outside. We lost the first litter that way, but the young mum was already pregnant again, unbeknownst to us, and she had a second litter before we could even blink. We shut the lot of them off in a designated kitten-room, while the snakes hung about outside. She had three babies this time around: one white and fluffy, one white with a black stripe, and one plain black with balding patches in front of her ears. I was waiting for them all to be old enough to be desexed, before giving them away, but I began to grow attached. The mother cat would go back to my son and his girlfriend, but perhaps I could keep one of the kittens? We had William, of course, that aloof tabby cat who always spurned my attentions, but surely I could have a cat who loved me back? The question then became: which one?

~

Post-desexing, we found a home for one of the kittens, but couldn't find it in us to give away the other two. The white fluffy kitten became fluffier, and the black one less baldy. We had never had a fluffy cat. In the forest, fluffiness was ridiculous.

'We can't keep the white one,' my mother would say, staring at him in amusement. 'He'll leave white fur everywhere!'

Once Milla and his girlfriend took the desexed mother cat back to their den, we brought the kittens into the main house. After a week or two, it dawned on us that we were keeping them both. We locked them up at night, but tentatively let them out briefly during the day, hoping they were now big enough to avoid the snakes. They darted about skittishly, the white fluffy cat so luminous, so conspicuous, there was no way he could creep up on birds or critters. William treated them with the same disdain he reserved for everyone, but the pup and the old dog were enthusiastic.

Kittens! they seemed to say, tails wagging, noses sniffing. How delightful!

—

My mother was the matriarch, so the pup slept under my mother's bed. I always got up early and Tully came out to greet me, sleepy-eyed and stretching, but he soon disappeared back under her bed. True morning began when my mother got up. Now it was breakfast time. First, he did the howl. The howl was aimed at my mother, but when she failed to act quickly enough, he would address the howl to me. My mother and I laughed in unison, heads thrown back. He was trying so hard to communicate, it was outright funny. The pup, frustrated by our laughing, would begin rallying the troops. He rounded up the three cats and the old dog and he herded them towards the kitchen.

It was breakfast time!

Didn't anybody know?

Bewildered, the other animals got in line as the pup hurried my mother, supervising the feeding carefully. Only once the others were all fed did he sit down to wait for his food. When the old dog had finished her bowl and come to sit by him, he finally began to eat. It seemed the pup was never actually hungry, but needed the encouragement of the old dog, sitting there, willing him to eat his meal. If Jet did not come, we had to call her in and station her nearby so Tully could begin to eat. Jet had always eaten anything at any time, so this strange morning routine took us by surprise. Tully was a working dog with no job, so moved through life inventing them.

~

Occasionally when I visited my lover, I intuited that he was impatient with my presence. It might have been that the relationship had reached the point where my lover was comfortable enough to sometimes find me irritating, but I didn't read it that way. I assumed, instead, that he had changed his mind about the whole thing and wished that I wasn't there at all. I became hypersensitive to the smallest slights, all the while hovering around him (as subtly as I could manage), hoping for signs of reassurance. He didn't give any. Or none that I could read. He still made me dinner and fussed over me, making sure my towel was warm and dry. He still rang if I was out, to check I was okay and not getting wet if it was raining. Yes, he was still attentive, but there was a tone of … detachment.

That dreaded word again!

In attachment literature, detachment was seen as a common 'deactivating strategy' used by avoidant attachers to suppress attachment or regulate closeness. Too much closeness or intimacy threatened their equilibrium. It was tricky territory because it meant that, unlike anxious attachers, whose focus on threats to intimacy made them hyper-aware of their own sensitivities, avoidant attachers could employ a whole host of deactivating strategies to quash or control intimacy, all the while remaining unconscious of their behaviours. What would register for them, instead, was the feeling of being smothered, and then, once enough distance had been created, a fresh desire for contact.

Attachment theory provided a framework for me to interpret my lover's cycles of closeness-withdrawal-closeness, but if he displayed too much detachment, I still began to unravel. I wanted to find a way to talk with him about these cycles, but was struggling against his lack of interest in the subject.

On the final night of one of my visits, I spoke up. 'Sometimes …' But that was as far as I got.

He looked across at me in the bed, a book in his hands.

'Yes?'

'It doesn't matter.'

I was aware that I only ever wanted to have a serious talk when it was late and he was exhausted. I knew it was a bad time. But truly, I believed that any time was a bad time for me to talk about my feelings, or his lack of them.

Frowning, he looked across at me. 'If you want to say something, do.'

I struggled to speak.

'Sometimes it's hard for me to tell if you like having me around.'

I couldn't look at him after uttering those words, so had no way of gauging his response.

He sighed, taking off his glasses. An elongated silence. 'Well,' he said finally, 'I guess I'm a pretty passive type of guy.'

Is that it? my mind screamed. Is that all you've got? I didn't respond, but rolled away from him indignantly.

My interpretation of his sentence: I am too passive to let you know in a straightforward way that I don't want you around. Curled up, eyes stinging, I nursed my hurt. He didn't offer any clarification, and I didn't ask him for any. The conversation ended there. Eventually he fell asleep, and I lay awake ruminating. If he was too passive to let me know that he didn't want to be involved with me, was it my job to end the relationship? I knew I didn't want to end it, but was it my responsibility? If I didn't end it, was I perpetuating my own mortification and humiliation? Was I harming myself by refusing to leave someone who couldn't love me but was too weak to make a break from me? Or, even worse, was I inflicting myself on someone who didn't in fact desire me? Was it a form of indecency? If I was a man, would I be considered pushy? Was I continually preferencing my own desire over his, without a care for how it affected him — just like my first boyfriend used to do to me?

In the morning, after he left for work, I wrote him a confused, tangential letter and left it under his pillow, then caught a taxi to the airport. My letter said nothing definitive except that I hoped he missed me — but I didn't say it as a threat. When I got home, I went about my normal business, still wrestling with what I saw as an ethical dilemma: whether or not it was my job to free him from me, when I didn't want him to be free.

~

Back home, Lou was visiting her parents at the family farm, so I popped around for a cuppa. Sitting at the kitchen table, the steam from our teacups rising, she asked me how my trip went, and, specifically, how it went with my lover. I told her about the last conversation we'd had, about his 'passive type of guy' statement. Repeating his words, I was tight-lipped with horror.

Lou listened in that way of hers: intuitive, subtle, wise.

'How did you interpret that?' she asked. 'What do you think he means?'

'That he's too passive to break it off with me,' I blurted. 'Of course!'

Lou had a crease between her brows that I sometimes caught her smoothing. How I loved her pensive frown.

'I don't think that's what he meant,' she said.

I was shocked. How else could that sentence be translated?

'I think he meant that he's not good at showing you how he feels,' she said matter-of-factly.

Lou's husband, Mike, came in from the next room and she put the question to him.

'Jess, I think you can assume this guy is interested in you,' he said. 'He calls you. He asks you to stay with him. He sends you gifts in the post. It's been over two years. If he didn't want to see you, he would *passively* avoid it.'

My world turned on its head. From my observations, Lou and Mike were classic secure attachers. They seemed to look at the world through a completely different lens from me. From their perspective, there was another possible interpretation. It mightn't be true, but an alternative way of looking at the situation existed. I made a promise to myself that I would ask my lover what he meant. I would behave like a secure attacher. I would ask him to clarify.

But I didn't. I still couldn't bear to hear his answer.

—

On my forty-first birthday my lover gave me a necklace. He handed me the small, neatly wrapped gift when we were still in bed, not long after waking. We had never spent a birthday together, and doing so this time was more coincidental than planned. I held the parcel, tentatively. I'm a rotten liar, and am often apprehensive opening a gift. Inside was a small linen pouch, and inside the pouch was the necklace. A long loop of tubular, finely-woven metal, painted in multicoloured patches, and only the colours I liked. I looked closely, trying to read this object's meaning, trying to gauge how to react. My lover's gesture — handing me the present — had seemed nonchalant, but I'd detected a hint of wariness. My heartbeat was jittery. Was he worried I would read too much into it? I was trying not to.

'Do you like it?' he asked.

I remained quiet, considering. There was something of the snake about the necklace, its graceful movement, and I liked how light it felt in my hands. Sections of it were painted gold. Because of the colours, it would match every piece of clothing I owned. I knew my lover had observed me closely to buy such a gift. It was like the embodiment of all my elements in one object. I liked it, and loved that he had chosen it, but I never wore necklaces. They made me feel as if I was choking.

'Yes, it's very unusual. So pretty.' I said eventually, wrapping it around and around my wrist. 'Maybe I can wear it like this?'

'However you like,' he said lightly.

~

Months later, in the city, a friend spied the necklace, wrapped around my wrist.

'I love this,' she said, touching it. 'That designer makes such great stuff.'

Designer? I struggled to remember the small linen pouch the necklace had come in. There'd been a name scrawled across it, but not one I'd recognised.

'He gave it to me, for my birthday,' I admitted. She knew about the older man, and that I stayed with him when I visited.

'Fancy!'

I did not know it was fancy.

'Does he let you call him your boyfriend yet?' She looked at me sideways, searching my face.

I shook my head.

'Jess,' she said, glancing down at the necklace, 'the boyfriend thing, he's just going to have to own it.'

I'd spent so long in the forest, I had no context to decode the language of gifts. Was this how it worked in the city? I was flying blind.

On the tram back to my lover's house I googled the designer, and blushed at the prices. Maybe the gold paint was real gold? Did it change the meaning of the gift? I just didn't know.

~

It had been almost three years since I'd made that first terrified phone call to the older man, yet I'd never mentioned to him that I was frightened of the phone. All the little things I never shared. It worried me that if my lover knew about my phone anxiety, the anxiety itself would move like a contagion and infiltrate his mind. But exposure to his phone calls had done its work. I'd begun to crave the sound of his voice on the other end of the line, and sometimes I even longed to call. It was easy for me not to act on my longing. My old phobia, the adrenaline rush I got from even picking up the phone, still skulked in the shadows, but I was surprised that the longing had, more or less, overcome the fear, and, occasionally, I could call.

On a quiet Sunday, the home phone rang. When I picked it up Lou was sobbing. Pete, her brother, was dead. Suicide. For the first few moments, as she tried to tell me the facts, all I could do was yell, 'No! No! No!' Then I went deaf. Lou was speaking, I heard her voice, but I couldn't hear what she was saying. I was crying by then too, shouting down the line, 'What? What? What?' As though my shouting would penetrate the deafness. Pete was the youngest of five. The baby. Bright like the sunshine. Beloved by us all. It took a few minutes for my hearing to return. Perhaps this is a somewhat normal response to such unbearable news, but it was the first time it had happened to me. A physiological obstruction to hearing the truth.

For three nights after Pete's death, Lou called me in the middle of the night and simply sobbed. I was alert at the first ring, my body charged, awake. Despite my readiness, all I could do was make a low, humming sound and listen to her cry, hoping I was in some way soothing her.

Once the wildness of the first grief calmed, Lou apologised.

'I'm so sorry to do that to you,' she said. 'I know how you are with the phone.'

After Lou's phone calls, my body began responding at night as though danger was lurking. I woke for no apparent reason, ready to run, pulling on clothes, without knowing where I was running to. It was like panic-induced sleepwalking. I loved Lou fiercely. She was a bright light in my life. I wanted to be the person she called when the worst thing possible happened, the person she called in the middle of the night. And wasn't life, at least partly, about learning how to manage the worst possible news? But my body had its own set of responses — idiosyncratic, uncontrolled.

~

When I was growing up, the farm, Lou's family home, was a refuge for me. Each of the five siblings often had friends over — the farm was always noisy, chaotic even, but in a vital, joyous way. I loved the farm more than I loved my own home. It had none of the complications of my homeplace, none of its dark history, but all of the pleasures: intimacy, connectedness, family, love and a winding creek-scape like no other.

After Pete's death, the family gathered at the farm, and Lou asked me to bring her some things she needed. Driving up the long driveway to the house, I felt panicked. My sister's suicide had been my father's breaking point. An event from which he couldn't recover. I was terrified that there was no other way Pete's death could go. More than anything, I wanted to be able to enter that beloved house and look into the eyes of each of Lou's siblings and say, 'I am so, so sorry.' I wanted to be able to show up for them, to bear witness to their pain. But I was afraid my own terror at the possible consequences of Pete's suicide would get in the way.

When I knocked on the front door, Lou's mother answered.

'Jess, these are the things that have helped,' she said, no preamble. 'Playing piano,' she counted them off on her fingers, 'listening to music.' She looked faintly feverish and I could feel my fear expanding.

Lou came to the doorway and kissed me on the cheek.

I stepped inside and they were all there, all except Pete. I wanted to be strong for them, but inside I was buckling. I tried to make my way around the room, sibling by sibling. But how could I look into so many shattered faces and find words? How does anyone do this? I was seizing up. What if this was their breaking point? What if there was no way to recover? Halfway round the room I became stranded, paralysed. I'd stepped into freeze. Lou's father had always watched his flock with an eagle eye, and when he saw me marooned, he picked his way across the room and wrapped his arms around me, his body soft with sudden, gentle sobbing.

'Aw, Jess,' he murmured. 'What can you do but cry?'

Something in me gave way and the stuckness released. We cried there together, the siblings watching. Through my tears I could see Lou's face. She looked calm, puffy from crying, but soft with surrender.

What could we do but cry?

—

There were hundreds of people at the funeral. All of us stunned, flat-faced.

The priest was a straight shooter.

'Pete's brain was on fire,' he said, looking around the room, meeting our eyes. 'He was just trying to put the fire out.'

The siblings and cousins carried the casket out on their shoulders to the waiting hearse. A strange stillness descended: the family, gathered around Pete's casket, and the rest of the mourners holding back, unsure whether to approach. It wouldn't be like this if he'd fallen off his horse, I thought, my body taut. People would know what to do. They would huddle, stay close. As the seconds ticked by, the gap between us and the family only seemed more unbreachable.

My mother, standing behind me, hissed in my ear, 'Jess, move forward!'

I nodded, but my body wouldn't obey.

Finally, a woman broke free and moved towards the family. An old primary-school friend of Lou's. That lone brave outlier! I wished it was me. Once she stepped forward, it broke the spell, and we all moved in unison, surrounding Lou's family with all our love and all our sorrow.

~

At the graveyard, the black cockatoos screeched wildly. The sky closed in, dark, squally, the cloud formations ludicrously cinematic. The brooding beauty seemed like an added blow. I winced at the unnecessary splendour, at the piercing bird calls all around us. At least the cockatoos knew how to echo the pain in our hearts! The family sat on seats under a small marquee set up next to the grave. Again, the rest of us hung back. Someone had made a playlist for Pete, and his young nieces and nephews, excited by the marquee and the music, danced to Coldplay next to the grave. That same invisible barrier kept the rest of us from approaching the family. We stood back in a wide crescent.

This time, the priest stepped up to fill the gap.

'Please,' he said, 'the family requests that you come forward if you wish to lay flowers.'

He motioned for us to approach the grave, but we were all pinned there, drowning in hesitation. My heart was banging so hard in my chest I could barely breathe.

'Come,' the priest beseeched, gesturing towards the grave with a sweep of his arm, 'please come.'

Slowly, like a terrified herd, we trickled forward.

Later, at the wake, Lou's mum said, 'Jess, he slipped through our fingers.'

She lifted her empty hands, holding them out in front of her, and I nodded. Lou's mum had held so many children steady, so many wayward teens. Her own kids and all of us ring-ins. Years and years of nurture. Years and years of love. How impossible it was to make sure you were holding everyone tight, all at once. That no one slipped free.

He slipped through our fingers.

My sister, Zoe, and Dad too.

I wanted to lie on the floor, right there, in defeat. I felt my hands clench at my sides, tight little fists. I was never letting go.

Unlike my psychiatrist father, who sought no professional assistance when Zoe took her life, Lou's father called in the big guns. For months afterwards, the family arranged group meetings with trained suicide grief counsellors. Sometimes Lou asked me to come and mind the kids.

One time, I had three kids under five, two of them Lou's and one her sister's. The plan was to drive down to the creek and keep them occupied until the group session was over. It was winter, so rather than swimming in the creek, we were fossicking along the banks. Lou's kids weren't used to being looked after by others, and I knew I needed to remain lighthearted in order to keep them there with me. If I let them walk ahead, I thought, they would feel like they were leading the way. We could spend hours collecting stones and insect carcasses, throwing them in the water, climbing around the giant roots of the trees along the creek bank.

A little way along, we stumbled on the camouflaged body of a desiccated newborn calf, its dry skin the same colour as the creek bank. It looked eerily like a sand sculpture. Mummified, but oddly perfect. This dead calf distressed me in a way that was difficult to conceal. I shooed the kids up the creek bank, pretending we hadn't seen the dead calf, but Iris, the oldest, was having none of it.

'I want Mummy!' she said, her lips trembling, her eyes wide.

'Let's just head up here,' I said, pointing aimlessly.

'No, I want Mummy!' she cried again, shaking her head, stamping a foot.

I had one job: to keep the kids occupied. I tried again to engage her attention.

'Look at this stick, it's a good shape!' I pointed at a curved stick on the ground and the other two little ones looked down at it obediently.

Iris stared at my face. 'I want Mummy!'

Abruptly, she was off and running, up towards the house.

I called after her, but she didn't stop. I started to chase her, before realising I had left the other two beside the creek.

'Shit,' I muttered. 'Shit! Shit! Shit!'

The little figure of Iris was racing across the paddocks towards the road that led to the house. It was a private road, but what if someone drove down and didn't see her? No one would expect a lone five-year-old to be hurtling along the road. I yelled out to her again, but I knew she wasn't listening.

'Come on!' I called to the other two. 'We better get her!'

We ran to the car and jumped in. I drove fast, trying to catch Iris before she got to the house.

Once the house was in view, I stopped the car and shot out to head her off at the pass. She busted into the lounge room — the group session — me hard on her heels.

One of Lou's siblings was speaking, her face so open and fragile that I looked away. This was a safe space, and we had broken in.

Lou scooped up Iris, hustling us both outside.

'I am so sorry,' I whispered. 'She got a fright.'

You only had one job, I thought. One. Fucking. Job.

'It's fine,' Lou said. 'I'll just put on a DVD.'

I gathered the other kids from the car and we all went into a bedroom to watch a movie. I was demoralised then. Iris's run had drained me of all authority, and I was worried I wouldn't be able to keep the kids in front of the DVD. Iris sat beside me, swinging her little legs. I kept thinking of the dead calf on the creek bank, and I kept thinking about Pete.

Suicides disrupt the equilibrium of entire communities. I'd experienced it with the death of both my sister and father, but I was still surprised by how much Pete's suicide affected me. It was a devastating loss, a shocking change, a wrenching separation, a tragedy beyond measure, but it was also a kind of reliving of the past. Lou's family, and the farm itself, had always had a magical, protective quality. A second home, but without any of the trauma. But now the trauma had come, the *same* trauma. The protective boundaries of the farm had been breached. The world felt unsteady. Was anywhere ever safe?

My lover was overseas when Pete died. In my grief, I'd emailed to tell him, unsure how to convey the immensity of this loss, the degree of devastation.

'How dreadful,' he'd written back. 'I'm sorry.'

What else could he say from the other side of the world?

After the dead calf, I got into a state, but I didn't know I was in a state until I called my lover and heard his voice on the other end of the line. He had returned from overseas, and I wanted to ask a quick question about my upcoming visit. He was eating dinner and said he would call back when he had finished. As soon as I put down the phone I was crying. A torrent of tears. Out of nowhere. I tried to rein in my crying, as I knew he would call back. And he did, faster than I expected. I went through the motions of asking the quick question, but my voice gave way, suddenly quavery. I didn't want to be this person crying on the end of the line. I pushed on, overcome, but unwilling to move into rawer territory. My lover knew I was a crier. I'd told him.

Sometimes, when I told him about an upsetting incident, he would ask, 'Did you cry?' knowing, I suppose, that I probably did.

Even though I was a crier, I rarely cried around him. Or not in the way that I was crying on the phone then. I felt ambushed by my own feelings. My lover was sympathetic, but I sensed his distance.

I tried to explain about the calf on the creekbank, shrunken and lifeless, but I wasn't making any sense. The calf had felt horrifically metaphoric, but in my distress I couldn't articulate it. I was offering up sentences that didn't go together. Snippets, interrupted by sobs. I knew my lover wouldn't hold it against me that I cried like this, that I spluttered so senselessly, but I was afraid he would love me less, if, indeed, he loved me at all. If he was considering breaking off with me, was I now pushing him over that edge?

This is being vulnerable, I thought, wanting to throw the phone at the wall. This is risking the possibility that I am unlovable in my raw state. This is being forced to find out.

'Tell me something better,' I said, desperate to change course.

He told me an anecdote from his day. I focused on his voice, trying to stem my rising fear.

I imagine all you secure attachers shaking your heads at my panic. You should be able to cry to your lover, you're saying. If he can't handle it, he's not worth it. Vulnerability is at the heart of intimacy and connection. Scraps of wisdom. My rational side knew them to be true. But in love I always felt on the brink of a precipice, on the threshold of abandonment and loss, trying to keep my footing, while remaining calm enough not to frighten away my beloved with the degree of my terror. Things were not going to plan.

—

I made a deal with myself that I wouldn't attempt to see my lover, that he had to attempt to see me. Our whole relationship had been built on a pattern of me initiating a trip to his city and then him initiating the time we spent together, but I wanted him to upend that pattern. I was testing if he might make the first move. I kept my lover in the dark. I waited for him to express a want to see me. He called me regularly enough and I was cheered by the sound of his voice, but he didn't suggest a visit. While I stuck to the deal, it filled me with regret. I was struggling to self-soothe. I thought I'd reached a place of immunity, trained myself to be more comfortable with uncertainty, with rejection. But since Pete's death, other parts of my world had become unstable. Emotional equilibrium was tougher to maintain.

I started swimming laps in the local pool to calm myself. I didn't know how to talk to anyone about what was distressing me. What could I say? I'm putting him through a test he doesn't know about and he's failing. His failure highlights his lack of motivation in regard to me. Anyone I told would say the same thing: you need to speak to him about it. I knew a secure attacher would not keep their lover in the dark. But, if I spoke to him, he might say the very words I didn't want to hear. Something along the lines of not wanting that kind of complication, of the whole thing being more than he'd expected. Once he said those words, how could I ignore them?

Without having that conversation, I could work up to phoning him, leave a message, and when he called me back forget that it wasn't him who initiated it. And we would have a nice conversation because he was a nice man. If I wasn't willing to ask outright, how could I know where I stood with a nice man? The mind boggles! How many relationships were held together by one person's unwillingness to hear the truth from the other? How many relationships continued simply because one person became expert at avoiding a conversation that might reveal the other person's ambivalence?

On the other hand, I could put him through my test, be aware of what his failing of the test might mean and still pursue our relationship, because I desired him, and his lack of interest in me wasn't as relevant to me as my own feelings. Was I then testing the limits of his passivity? How far could I push before he would push me away? Sometimes falling in love with someone was the most selfish act on earth. The feelings so monstrous and consuming you'd prioritise them over all else, even the person at the centre of the feelings. And you'd delude yourself that this was your gift to them, because: love.

~

Losing Pete had intensified my hypervigilance, so I tried to balance out my fear by tracking, once again, the ways my lover and I were close. Instead of focusing on the gaps between us, I forced myself to run through all our moments of connectedness. Not just the sex, but all the time he'd spent in my company. Walking his neighbourhood streets. Sitting together in restaurants. Swimming in his ocean. The way he always wrapped an arm around me when a movie became violent. I assembled the things he'd shared with me — his thoughts, his feelings. The times, in the back of a crowded winter bar, sipping a drink, surrounded by the clatter of other people, he'd tell me a snippet from his past and turn teary, and I'd rest my hand on his thigh. All those moments of attunement, surely they counted?

~

In calmer periods, I wondered if what I interpreted as detachment or lack of interest might be my lover going through his own bad time. Ever since we'd met, I'd sensed an ever-present air of melancholy about him, which he seemed to keep from dipping into a full-blown existential crisis through his dedication to enjoying the little things in life. Breakfast: he took such joy in it. A cup of well-brewed tea: oh, the loveliness! I watched him keenly in these moments, certain there was something for me to learn. I admired the way he would murmur to himself and turn a rotten situation around. It was part of what I enjoyed about his company: his daily efforts to keep the black dog at bay. Despite his habits of happiness, he was probably not immune to slipping into darkness and despair from time to time. Unfortunately, he was not the type to say so, and it was hard for me to tell. So there we were: me spinning on an axis of abandonment and sorrow and rage; him keeping to himself, presumably oblivious to my feelings. How to get off that runaway train?

My lover seemed so self-contained, so impenetrable. But there had been times between us when this impenetrableness seemed to drop away. I thought back to an evening when I had been out in his city, catching up with friends. He had encouraged me to go, as though it was nothing to him, but when I got back to his house, latish, he was still up. We sat on the couch together, side by side. I was quiet — tired, overstimulated.

'Have you already gotten sick of me?' he said, face tilting towards me, forlorn.

'No,' I said, 'nothing like that.'

I kissed him then, even though in that moment I would have preferred to be alone. He had needed it, and I knew what it was like to need.

And then it happened — he began to phone me less often. And when he did, all I sensed was his impatience. He was busy, he was bored. He couldn't wait to get back to whatever he was doing. It was hard to tell if he was still borderline polite, because I was so overwhelmed by his tone of dismissal. Was this the way our relationship would stumble to a halt? Him responding to me with more and more coldness, until I finally froze over. I resolved never to call him again. Who wants to be frozen out? I wondered, and not for the first time, why my feelings regarding him remained so constant, while his feelings ebbed and flowed? I didn't want to tie it to my crying on the phone — surely that was not a criminal offence after you had been seeing someone for three years? But the idea hung there: that I'd been vulnerable, needy, and he had withdrawn.

What did I do, faced with the withdrawal of his affection? My body seized up with pain. My chest hurt — heart hurt! I lost pleasure in the simple things. I began to dread an oncoming depression. I got my blood tested, convinced I had an iron deficiency. I tried to make an extra effort with my health. I cuddled the dogs and cats more than they were happy about. And all the while, I was bewildered that something with so much promise, something I'd developed faith in, could just shrivel to nothing.

~

When faced with the dimming of my lover's interest, it was tempting to believe that if I did a particular thing, he would respond in a particular way; that cause and effect was at play rather than a simple failure to thrive. But sometimes even the most lovingly tended plant simply dies. In my sensitised state, I believed my lover's detachment was his way of wilfully starving any feelings he may have had for me. It was the message I got from his offhand phone manner and I was quick to extrapolate. Inside me, a silent fury grew in response to what I perceived as his coldness. I understood that my lover was not obliged to keep his feelings for me alive. He had made no promises. He had never pretended he was either willing or able. He owed me nothing. Nevertheless, I was angry.

~

According to my 500-page book on attachment theory, babies are born with instinctual 'relationship-seeking' patterns of behaviour — sucking, clinging, following, crying and smiling — all rooted in the fact that proximity to the mother, because essential to survival, is also *satisfying*. For a baby or young child, proximity brings joy; conversely, a lasting or untimely disruption to proximity creates anxiety, grief, and depression. How does a baby or young child typically react to disruptions in proximity? Protest, despair and detachment — the three key emotional experiences that later govern our psychology in matters of the heart. 'Protest is an embodiment of separation anxiety, despair is an indication of mourning, detachment a form of defence.' Oh, how clearly the pattern of our love played out in that sentence. With all my self-soothing, I had given up protest, but I was well acquainted with despair. My lover, it seemed, was stuck at detachment. Would this dance ever change?

—

I continued to resist contacting my lover and he continued to call me. Less often than I would have liked to talk to him, but, nonetheless, he became the one initiating all contact. He seemed to have no idea about my emotional turmoil, and I was pretty sure from his phone manner that he was not experiencing any of his own in regard to me. Which was good, in the sense that he (perhaps) thought the matter of our relationship was more settled than he let me know, and bad, in that (perhaps) he simply didn't think about me much at all. Oh, the awfulness of being the one who is not thought of! The terrible unevenness of love.

Of course, it is unlikely, if not ludicrous, to imagine that two lovers would think of each other in an equally obsessive way all the time, or even some of the time. But it was a blow to realise that I'd wasted a monstrous amount of mental energy. My lover had probably used his for other passions: his work, his friend-ships, his children, rearranging the pictures on his walls, reading books, watching movies, enjoying the city skyline. All the mind-space he had used to entertain thoughts that were not about me! How I envied him that. To be so free!

—

I gave up waiting for him to initiate a visit. Results from my testing had been unambiguous: our in-person relationship existed only through my initiation. I was the instigator. I'd always been the instigator. That was the pattern of our exchange. He was passive, I was active. But I'd given him plenty of opportunity to passively avoid me, to stop calling, to let the relationship fizzle, and he had not. I booked some flights, and he sounded pleased that I was coming. Maybe that was enough?

~

That visit, I was shrouded in a cloud of sadness. My lover seemed to keep me at bay. He still enacted all his rituals of hospitality, but I felt there was a part of himself he was removing from me — holding aloft — and that was the part I most wanted to see. Walking the streets while he was at work, I teared up intermittently. I felt angry at his withdrawal, but I was also angry at myself. Had I done the same thing I always did: grown unwieldly, unwanted feelings for someone who simply wished I hadn't?

Like my lover, I was a master at avoiding confrontation, but after a couple of days veering between sadness and rage, I sat down beside him on the couch and finally cracked.

'Why do you call me and then sound cross?'

He seemed surprised. He was clearly not aware of his phone manner.

'Well …' he paused. 'I call you on Sundays, when I know you'll be home.'

'You sound like you feel obliged to call, but you don't really want to talk.' Now that I'd started here, I was stuck. 'That doesn't feel good for me.'

'Well, I'm not going to call you every day.'

No! I didn't want him to call me *more* often. I was happy for him to call me *less* often, but to call me as if he meant it.

'That's not what I want,' I said, already frustrated.

'Well, I've always been shit on the phone.'

'Yeah, I'm shit on the phone too.'

I still hadn't mentioned my longstanding phone phobia.

'I guess what's bothering me is the discrepancy between our feelings,' I said. 'It's this thing I do …' I'd never spoken to him of my attraction to ambivalent men. He probably thought I talked all the time, but I never told him any of the things that really mattered.

He was utterly still.

Finally, he looked at me sideways, his gaze unusually direct. 'I'm not in love with you, if that's what you mean.'

Even though I'd initiated the conversation, I was shocked by his words. I felt my face fill with heat, my belly begin to churn. That was not the response I had expected. I would never ask someone if they were 'in love' with me.

'And I don't want to get married or — you know — move in together,' he added, somewhat unnecessarily. 'I mean, even if that were possible, I don't think it would be a good idea.'

Although I'd never wanted to get married or live with him, my feelings were so hurt by this statement, it felt like a punch to the face.

'But I am very fond of you and I like you very much.' He put a hand on my leg and gave it a light squeeze. 'You are wonderful.'

I was trying with all my might not to cry.

Sensing my distress, my lover said, with some conviction, 'I mean, I do love you.'

Things had got out of hand. My heart was banging in my chest. I wanted to get up and run, but I was repressing that urge too.

'Is it important to you?' I asked. 'Do you want to be in love? Do you want to get married?'

For someone who avoided these kinds of conversations even more actively than I did, my lover seemed remarkably calm.

'Not particularly,' he said. 'No.'

'Sometimes I think you want me to find someone else,' I said.

'No,' he replied, with some force. 'I'd be very sad if you did that.' He crossed his arms over his chest. 'Very jealous.'

That was more upfront than I'd expected.

I told him then of my four-years-of-unrequited-love-hell. I told him that I sometimes saw that man on the streets of my hometown, that I always cried when I spoke to him, and that the man just thought I was the type who cried easily. I cried as I told my lover, because it was easier to cry about the last man I'd loved, and not him. I told my lover that I always chose people who wouldn't be able to love me. I told him that being 'in love' was not something I aimed for. I told him that I'd never wanted to be a wife.

He looked relieved.

'So when you climbed onto my lap that first time, is that what you were thinking? He's perfect. He definitely hasn't got it in him.'

My belly was still roiling. I was still fighting back tears.

'Maybe …' I said, without really believing it.

I'd known my lover was ambivalent, but I hadn't equated that with him being incapable of falling in love. All the sensation I normally experienced in my lover's presence was seeping from me. I climbed onto his lap in an attempt to retrieve the feeling. He placed his hands gently on my breasts, over my shirt, and I cupped my hands over his.

'Well, that's alright, then,' he said softly. 'Neither of us is in love.'

I wanted more than anything for it to be that simple. I looked down at his hands on my breasts. Hands that I'd loved from the outset, on breasts that he once claimed were magnificent.

'I didn't say that.' I couldn't stop myself from speaking. 'Just that being in love isn't the most important thing for me.'

Did he understand? We sat in stillness, me cupping his hands, him cupping my breasts.

After a long silence he said, 'Well, there are two things we can do. Go to bed, or you can help me chop vegetables for dinner.'

I had no feeling left in my body, but I wanted us to go and fuck. Maybe the feeling would come back? This time he came the way I usually did, all shuddery tremors. I couldn't come at all. Numbness had taken over, and even his skilful hands couldn't bring the sensation back. We got up and I watched him chop vegetables and then we caught a tram into town to see a movie. In the dark theatre, I began to feel a sense of rising nausea. A steel ring was tightening around my skull. I knew what it meant — a migraine was on its way. If I was at home, I would take pain-killers and lie in the dark. In the cinema, I was paralysed.

While we waited for the tram home, my lover tried to avoid a female acquaintance. He had never done that before. Was he troubled to be seen with me? Was she someone he would prefer didn't know about us? The woman spotted him and they exchanged greetings. On the tram, the three of us sat together and the woman talked about her new dog. The ring around my skull was tightening further, pressing against my eyes. The woman talked and talked and I could tell that my lover found her annoying. He was usually so tolerant, but she clearly got under his skin. So, he was not, after all, ashamed to be seen with me? As the woman chattered, I worried I might suddenly vomit. I broke out in a cold sweat. Finally, the woman got off at her stop.

'I feel really ill. Migraine coming,' I said to my lover. 'I don't know if I'll make the walk home.'

He watched me calmly. I mustn't have looked as bad as I felt. We got off the tram. The pain was hovering, ready to pounce, but it was only a short walk home. I tried to breathe slowly and deeply. At the front door, the pain caught me. My lover unlocked the door and I careened towards the bedroom, pulling off my jeans, then my shirt. Blinded, I climbed under the covers.

'Help me with my bra,' I commanded.

Everything was unbearable. The bra was like the ring around my skull, squeezing me so tight it hurt. I turned my back towards him and he grappled with the clasp. My eyes were shut, I couldn't see him, but I sensed the moment he understood the agony I was in.

He stood beside the bed, 'Can I do anything else?'

'Get me a bucket.' I was crying, hot, gulping, unstoppable tears. 'And maybe a cold washer.'

He fetched the bucket and the washer. I covered my eyes. I'd started to sob. 'Please, I'll be okay.' My words were coming out jumbled. 'Just leave me — I need to be in the dark for a while.'

I felt him linger a minute, and then he was gone.

'Fuck, fuck, fuck,' I moaned. It was the pain, of course, but it was also the horrible realisation that I'd done it again. I'd fallen in love with someone who simply didn't, and wouldn't, love me in return. I'd done so wilfully, forcefully. I'd been stupid and selfish and wildly deluded. All the sensations — the burning hurt, the squeeze of containment, the pressure created by keeping my feelings in — I remembered them all from the last time.

'Fuck, fuck, fuck!' I hoped my lover couldn't hear me.

I heard whimpering, soft and mournful. It sounded faraway, but it was coming from me. As the pain subsided, I fell quiet. I pulled the washer from my face and turned onto my side.

My mind was empty.

When the pain had finally gone, I dressed and went to the kitchen. He had made dinner.

'I think I should eat something,' I said. 'Maybe it will help?'

He served us both a plate of food. Without the pain, every pleasant sensation was heightened. I could feel each grain of rice separately on my tongue. I chewed slowly, marvelling at the taste. I knew my lover was watching me. I glanced up at his face. It was the saddest I had ever seen it.

It's okay, I wanted to say. It was only a migraine.

But we both knew that it was not.

~

Migraines swallow time. Often I wouldn't remember with any precision the hours before or the hours after. My lover took me back to bed and curved his long body around my small frame. He held me tight. I remembered the conversation we had on the couch. I remembered what I'd said and what he'd said, but, lying in bed, I was becoming less and less certain that we'd truly understood each other.

'I feel a little unclear,' I whispered. 'About what we talked about.'

My lover was silent, but the room seemed to fill with his rising alarm.

'Maybe we should talk about it again?' I added.

Immediately, I felt the hint of the ring around my skull contracting.

'I really don't think we should,' he said shakily. 'Not now, anyway.'

'Okay,' I said. 'You are right.'

In the morning, I was subdued. He would go to work and I would fly home. The remnants of the migraine had stolen my words. I remained silent, at sea.

My lover's face had not lost its sadness.

He got ready, his pottering morning routine. I sat on the couch, unmoving. Before he left, he came and knelt at my feet. He laid his head in my lap, wrapped his arms around my waist. For a few minutes he stayed like that, and I felt all his tenderness and kindness and love — and yet I understood nothing. He was not in love with me. I was forty-one years old, but I was a child. When would I grow up?

—

Back home, my mother picked me up from the airport, and I cried as soon as I climbed into the car.

'It's okay,' I said through gushing tears. 'It's not over.'

I wondered if there was a limit to the amount of unlovedness I was willing to tolerate, but I didn't say that. My mother listened to me cry in that quiet way of hers. She enjoyed difficult men. But did she think this degree of difficulty too much?

—

If I had rejected the idea of marriage or partnership, what was left? I already had a family. Big and boisterous and growing. My mother and my sons and their girls and the dogs and the cats and the forest. I did not want to build a new family with someone I desired, and I did not particularly want to bring my desired person into the family I already had. I simply wanted to explore my desire, and to spend time (but not too much time) in the presence of my desired person. I did not want to argue over whose turn it was to cook or clean. I did not want to see my desire dissipate in the face of familiarity or everyday resentments. I wanted to be a cherished occasional guest in the house of my lover. I did not want to overstay my welcome. I did not want to begin to find my lover ordinary or irritating. I did not want to become slowly unseen or taken for granted. I had prioritised desire over the longevity or stability of the relationship. But I did not desire anyone else. My desire was specific to my lover. I was fixed in my attentions, although I wished my body would open to the possibility of others. I wished I wasn't a flower turned only towards the sunshine of his touch. I wished I desired women. I wished my body wasn't so easily triggered. I wished I needed less safety. I'd tried hard to be brave, but I'd used up so much courage acting on my desire for the older man, now I was tired, worn out. I'd begun dreaming of all the ways I was unloved by him, sometimes jumping up in terror at night and running down the stairs. Outside, in the forest, stranded in the blackness of night, I would startle awake, shaking with fear, unsure of where I was running, or what I was running from. My fight or flight response was activating in my sleep, like it had in the first weeks after Pete's death.

I didn't know how much more stress my body could stand. My eyes began to play up, the tissue around them swollen and sore to the touch. No matter how much I rested them, I couldn't bring the swelling down.

Was my experiment coming to an end? Should I choose to live without this outlet for my desire? Or choose someone less ambivalent, who I'd no doubt desire less. I would have to de-prioritise desire altogether, so I could get some unbroken sleep.

—

Saturday morning, I was hanging out at Nika's house. We had been on and off laughing all visit. I was sitting in the corner chair and she was standing in the kitchen.

'Jess, there's something I have to tell you,' she said, her tone abruptly authoritative.

For a second, I was all animal terror. A wide-eyed glance of fear at her face. My body frozen, locked.

'Oh no,' Nika said. 'I saw that.'

I looked down at my lap, caught out.

'Jess, I only wanted to tell you how I make the porridge you like,' she said worriedly, pointing at the breakfast bowls she had laid out.

I felt strangely ashamed, as though shame was an odd by-product of unnecessary terror.

'Did you think you were getting in trouble?' she asked.

I stood and walked over to the kitchen, trying to recover. We were standing face to face, the floating kitchen counter between us.

'No,' I whispered, looking down at the bowls. 'I thought someone was dead.'

It was the least rational possibility. The two of us had been hanging about together since the night before; if something terrible had happened to someone we loved, she would have already told me, but my body didn't know that. A traumatised body jumped to conclusions. A traumatised body was always on high alert. A traumatised body was stiff and sore from the strain of its watchfulness. A traumatised body forgot how to right itself. My body had simply registered the seriousness of Nika's voice, the announcement quality, and gone — in less than a second — from 0 to 100 stress. Fight or flight mechanism, or for me — freeze.

I looked up at Nika's face and her eyes filled with tears.

'I saw that,' she said again. 'That's trauma.'

'I know,' I said, and the frozen energy in my body suddenly thawed. I began, against my will, to weep.

She came around the counter and held me.

This is closeness, I thought. This is love.

~

Every day I was with my father, he told me he loved me. Emphatic, determined. After his suicide, that love felt untrustworthy. Ever since then, I watched actions, read expressions, favoured the unspoken over words. People say all sorts of things they want to believe.

~

My lover called, checking in. I had refrained from contacting him, wondering if he would just let the relationship fizzle, but he hadn't. We didn't speak about his 'not in love' revelation. We chatted about the books we were reading and the films we'd seen, though there was something different in his tone, a kind of alertness. As if he was waiting, primed for defence. But I did not attack. What could I say? He had a right to be not in love. He had a right to tell me. He had said it wasn't important to him. He had said that he loved me. The tricky part — for me — was figuring out how much the difference between being 'in love' or simply 'loving' mattered.

~

I went to a writers' retreat in the mountains. Five of us, strangers, stayed there for two weeks. There was a younger woman, sparky and clever, bright with promise. I loved her unequivocally from the beginning. With all the communal dinners, intimacy was fast-tracked. We two talked and talked about our lives. The younger woman read my memoir, *Staying*, in her non-writing hours on the retreat.

When I told her about my lover, about his ambivalence, she said, 'Has this man read your memoir?'

I nodded.

'And he still treats you like that?'

I laughed.

She is young enough, I thought, to believe that would make a difference.

~

At the writers' retreat, we talked about ethics. The ethics of writing about other people. My new young friend said, 'He deserves it. Whatever you've written, he deserves it.' But not everyone was so sure.

I wasn't.

Writing about my relationship with the older man was like conducting a secret second life — potentially hurtful, potentially damaging of trust. I'd been engaged in the act of writing about him from the first time I'd met him. I needed the writing in order to hold my nerve. I needed to have somewhere to express all the confusion and bewilderment I was afraid would spill over and destroy whatever tenuous bond was being built. I never believed our relationship was solid enough to withstand the kind of intensity I would bring to it if I didn't have a writing outlet.

Even though the older man was aware that I was writing about our relationship, I was certain he'd have no inkling of what the writing was like. It would be impossible for him — a deeply private person — to conceive of what I was creating. A part of me was always waiting for this secret second life to be found out.

I feared that when I finally gave my lover this memoir, he would break up with me, or that the only way I could share it with him was as part of a breakup I instigated. A friend told me that in Norwegian folklore, if you knit a jumper for your boyfriend, he will leave you. Was my writing that knitted jumper? A break-up-inducing gift. Knitted over the years. Knotty, complex, sometimes beautiful. As long as we were still in a relationship, I couldn't finish what I was writing without finishing the relation-ship — I was writing a book I never wanted to end.

~

The next time I visited my lover the storm had passed.

'We muddle through,' he said when I arrived. A kind of acknowledgment.

Tentative hope took root inside me.

He bought tickets to the theatre. I'd never been to the theatre, and imagined it full of sophisticated women in fur coats, though I hoped I was wrong. After some deliberation, I wore a dress I'd bought especially for his city — light grey, made from a fine knitted wool, seamless. It was tight, with a high neck. Elegant but also busty. At home I'd been experimenting with wearing the necklace he gave me. It was so light and long, it didn't give me the choking feeling I usually had with necklaces.

'Nice frock!' he said when he saw me. High praise! 'And you're wearing my necklace.'

I was pleased that he was pleased.

The theatre was a more public outing than we usually opted for, and I was nervous. We caught a tram into the city. It was opening night, brimming with people.

He scanned the crowd.

'There're some friends of mine just over there.' He pointed. 'Do you want to say hello?'

I am wearing a very tight dress, I thought, blushing. I hadn't imagined meeting friends of his at the theatre. He had given me no warning.

'Sure,' I said, hoping my cheeks were not as pink as they felt.

We approached, and he introduced me as his 'friend'. The two couples seemed to gawp at me. He has told no one about me, I thought. I have arrived out of nowhere. In a very tight dress.

I did my best to make small talk, but it is not one of my strengths.

I was relieved when the announcement came for us to take our seats, which were a few rows down from his friends. I sensed them watching us settle. When I turned around, one of them waved. I wasn't imagining their interest.

The curtains parted and the play began. It was warmer inside than I'd expected. Under the grey dress I had on tights and a light thermal skivvy — I was overheating. When I got too hot, I often coughed. I could feel the dry itch at the back of my throat. The theatre was hushed, and I tried swallowing hard to supress the cough. I concentrated on breathing evenly, trying to focus on the show.

My lover did not even pretend to watch the play; he watched

my face instead, gauging my responses. With his friends behind us, I was being watched being watched. I hoped I was responding appropriately, although the play seemed oddly hollow, lacking in some essential vitality, not quite alive. In contrast, my lover's attention to my reactions made my body tingle. It's probable that his interest was adding to my heat. He couldn't not be 'in love' with me if my face was more entrancing to him than the play. That's what I was thinking, while I stifled my cough. He says he isn't in love with me, but he is a liar.

At intermission, I fled to the toilets to shed the tights and skivvy, while my lover got us drinks. I looked in the mirror of the theatre bathroom, and saw that without the skivvy the dress was almost sheer. I, a forest-dwelling hermit, had never felt so on display, and now I was dressed in a sheer, tight dress, my breasts visible bouncing shadows beneath the grey fabric.

This is … unfortunate, I thought, pressing my skivvy and tights into my handbag.

Back at our seats, he gave me my wine, and I turned and smiled at his friends, who were still watching us.

'What do you think?' he asked. 'Are you enjoying it?'

I didn't know how to express the complexity of my thoughts at that point. 'Yes, yes,' I said instead. 'It's fun. I like the staging.'

He seemed satisfied with my answer. After the play was over, and after more small talk with his friends at the opening-night drinks, where I warded off indelicate questions about our 'friend-ship', and we finally escaped into the freezing night air, I looked across at my lover and laughed.

'You could have warned me,' I said. 'That all your friends would be there!'

This sudden introduction to the other parts of his life. As though we were a couple.

He glanced down the length of me, in my sheer grey dress, as I stood there under the street lamp.

'It was okay, wasn't it?' he said finally, running a hand through his hair.

I smiled, and breathed in the cold city air, breathed it deep into my lungs. Cool down, I willed myself. You can cool down.

—

Back at his house, we fucked. Easily, joyfully. Inhabiting our imperfect, damaged bodies. Afterwards, he walked down the hallway, naked, to put on the kettle. I lay on the bed and thought of the fireflies back home. How they glinted through the forest at dusk in spring, otherworldly, their light intermittent, pulsing. Flashes of impermanence, disappearing into the night. It was hard to encounter them and not feel a sense of wonder, a sudden tightening of the chest. And then I thought of my lover, naked and pouring water into the teapot. His beautiful, tapered fingers.

Sex and a cup of tea, I thought. My favourite kind of day.

fireplan

Each day we hear of new catastrophes. Floods. Fires. Thousands of fish suddenly dead in the rivers. Mass insect extinctions. And yet our lives go on. We run out of milk and go to the shops. We think about what to make for dinner. We make plans, including holidays. We coast through whole days on social media. We love our children fiercely. We pat our cats and walk our dogs. Meanwhile, we feel the effects of a dying planet. There is too much rain. Our seasons shift. Summer comes a month late, winter too. There is no rain. The mosquitos, usually ubiquitous, disappear. It is hot like it has never been hot. It is hot like it has never been hot for many days in a row. And yet, among these daily reminders that the world is undergoing unprecedented change, we can still spend all our waking moments obsessing about whether or not our lover truly loves us. The absurdity of it is bizarre. The absurdity isn't lost on me.

—

When I first entered the four-years-of-unrequited-love-hell, my mother's partner, Shawn, was dying. My mother met Shawn after the death of my father, and he'd been a reliable, nurturing presence in our lives ever since. When Shawn first got his cancer diagnosis, I couldn't stop crying. He and my mother were calm. I was a tap left running that was slowly flooding the house. I kept thinking, this time I'll have time. This time I can do it right. There was nothing I wanted more than to be with this beloved man in his final days. Except that I didn't. It took three years for Shawn to die, and during that time I became more and more frightened of being in the room with him. As his sickness progressed, my obsession with my unrequited-love-object grew. In my everyday life, I watched my father-figure slowly deteriorate, while, in an alternate reality, my fantasy life exploded. I knew that I was escaping from the awfulness of saying goodbye, from the obvious re-triggering that losing this man was engendering, but I still couldn't rein in my obsessive-compulsive fixation on my unwilling love interest.

The last time I saw Shawn, I stood at the edge of the room, unable to enter. He watched me from his perch on the couch, bald as a baby bird, slack-faced but serene. I swiped at my tears angrily.

Do it, I urged myself. Tell him how much you love him.

But I couldn't say a word.

He peered at me, all gentleness, no judgement.

I get it, his eyes seemed to say. Jess, it's okay.

When Shawn finally breathed his last breaths, I was in

another city, chasing the promise of the unwilling man. Crazy with denial, crazy from blocking out the oncoming grief. Shawn died the night before I got home, and all I could say was, 'I don't understand. I'm not ready.' My obsession with love had blinded me so completely, I couldn't see death at the door.

All through the day it felt like sunset. We walked outside cautiously, expecting brimstones to go with the fire. The dogs wouldn't come on their daily walks. The cats were on alert, darting outside to look at the sky, but racing back in to hide under the couches. Fires burned all around us. Binna Burra, where I'd gone as a forest-dwelling child to see the true rainforest, had been taken by the flames. Further north and south there were mass evacuations. We worried that if the power went down, as often happened even in ordinary weather, we'd have no wi-fi and no way of receiving emergency warnings. We were submerged in a rainforest in a valley — we couldn't see anything on the horizon. If there was no power, we would have no water, as our household water system relied on electric pumps. And if our dead-end road was blocked by fire, or even fire trucks, we had no way out. It had never occurred to us to have a fireplan. There had never been fires before. The smell of smoke in the air was ever-present. It was only September, but it was bone dry. The light turned, eerie, unearthly. Was this how you knew the apocalypse was coming?

In this new reality where we needed a fireplan, I approached the local fire brigade for advice. I suspected my homeplace was undefendable, which meant leaving early was Plan A, but it was important to have a Plan B. The local fire service held an information day, which I attended with some apprehension. At these community gatherings, I always felt on the outside. I'd lived in this town most of my life, but was conscious that my family history had left me perpetually estranged. It had been over twenty years since the suicides, but the feeling had never really lifted.

As I got out of my car, I scoped the gathered crowd for familiar faces, but didn't see any. Mostly the firefighters were men in dirty yellow uniforms, sweaty-faced and slow-moving inside the bulk of their fireproof outfits. Their answers to my questions (anxieties) were offhand, somehow inarticulate. Was I not asking the right questions? I felt as if I was engaged in a dance to which I didn't know the steps. Something to do with introductory chat, a way of easing into a conversation, whereas I always went the direct route. I didn't know the dance, and nervousness made me forthright. My directness seemed to elicit indirectness, which increased my sense of disorientation. The men pointed me towards the shed and told me I should ask 'the boss'.

The boss was a woman close to my mother's age. I remembered her from primary school. Somebody's mother. Her child had been asthmatic, and she was particularly tender with him.

As a kid, I'd loved her from afar. I explained my circumstances and my anxiety to her.

I watched her gaze flicker over my face.

'You been here a long while?' she said. 'I know your face.'

She was claiming me, I could feel it. I said my mother's name.

'And your father was Ian?'

No one ever said his name.

I nodded. You got me, I wanted to say.

'I'll come and check out your house,' she said. 'There's a few of you we're worried about. Dead-end roads, or roads we can't get the truck down. I'll come and see.'

I wanted to cry then and there. Someone was worried about us! Someone would come and see! Someone had said my father's name out loud. Someone had seen I belonged.

—

The woman from the fire brigade came, as promised. She climbed down out of her ute, looking stiff and sore. When she saw my mother, her face lit up.

'You haven't changed a bit,' she said. 'Always were—' she seemed to search for words, but gave up, shaking her head. I assumed she wanted to say some variant of 'beautiful' but I couldn't be sure.

My mother raised herself onto the balls of her feet, a subtle movement she always executed when receiving a compliment. Neither of us could say the woman hadn't changed. Dusty, dry, scorched around the edges, she looked like she'd battled a million fires.

The woman gazed at the garden forest towering around us.

'Well, I can see this is a life's work,' she said. 'You done good. It looks amazing.'

My mother and I smiled, but we knew what was coming.

She walked around the perimeters of the house, admiring the garden.

'You cleaned the gutters,' she said. 'That's good.'

I tried not to show how much her praise pleased me. Cleaning our gutters was a difficult job: each building had a separate gutter, and I'd cleaned them all. I probably executed a toe-rise at the compliment too.

'Look,' she said finally. 'Before, we would have said rainforest like this was a fire deterrent.' She gazed again at the canopy above us. 'But these fires now, they're doing all sorts of different things. They're unpredictable. You saw what happened up at Binna Burra. We never thought we'd see anything like that.'

Once, our forest would have been an asset. Now it was a liability.

The woman from the fire brigade pointed out some simple things we might change to make the place safer, and she told us where we should try to shelter on the property if we got trapped.

'The biggest thing is, you got to get to know your neighbours,' she said, a parting piece of advice. 'Someone round here's gotta have a safer spot than this.'

Mum and I glanced at each other. We were both bona fide

hermits. We had no idea which properties around us were safer. No idea how to find out.

The woman climbed back into her ute and wound down the window.

'It's real beautiful,' she said, looking at my mother. 'But you gotta get out early.'

~

Without any warning, our old dog couldn't walk or even stand. Jet was large and heavy, so we slung towels beneath her belly to move her, a person on each side. We took her to the vet — the red-haired one, not the handsome one — but he couldn't diagnose anything without running a battery of tests, and she was too old for that.

'Don't leave her longer than a week in that condition,' the vet advised, before sending us home.

In the days that followed, we shifted her from inside to outside in the towel sling, trying to give her the pleasure of the grass and the sky and the wind. Once out, she sniffed the smoky air sadly. All the cats settled themselves around her on the grass like sentinels. The young pup licked her face. Tully alone remained chipper, the only one who didn't seem to know what was coming. Luca started sobbing in his bedroom. He sobbed for days, though he stopped periodically to help us carry her inside and out. Milla was subdued. In this countdown to death, my younger son was doing all the grieving. Usually it was me. On the sixth day, the old dog's belly began to swell. She seemed so mournful, so tired. The cats gathered around her, even closer.

~

When I told Lou that Jet was dying, she said, 'You know you'll need a very deep hole for the grave.' Lou was a farm girl and she knew about death. Our soil was clay. Digging a hole to plant even a small tree required some stamina. I knew my sons could dig a deep hole, but they had sore backs, and jobs, and it would take an age to dig a hole that deep. While I'd been silently worrying, my mother had come up with a plan. When Luca was a child, he was obsessed by the idea of building a bunker. My mother allocated him a spot, far out of sight, down on one of the flats, surrounded by decrepit old fruit trees, and he spent weeks digging. Was he trying to claim some space for himself in the wild tangle of histories that was his birthplace? Recreate the world down his hole? Of course, the soil was unforgiving and he was a child, so though he dug for weeks, his hole was too small for a bunker. The allure of his fantasy fell away. I'd long forgotten about his mission, but my mother hadn't. We went to find the hole. It was deep, and exactly the size of the old dog.

~

A different vet, an ex-neighbour, came to the house to help our old dog die. This vet looked stiff, pained, his hips and knees in a terrible state. Slowly, he lowered himself down.

'You can hold her in your arms,' he said, signalling to us.

She was so heavy, we knew we couldn't lift her. Instead, we surrounded her, our hands resting on her, willing her to feel our love. He gave her the injection and the life ebbed out of her. Agitated, Tully circled her body, his ears pricked up in confusion. He sniffed around us, looking at our faces, searching our eyes for meaning. There was none to be found. What had we done?

As Luca helped us manoeuvre Jet's dead body into the hole, he dry-retched. Weak stomachs run in the family on his father's side.

'I think I handled that pretty well,' he said archly, sly self-deprecation his specialty.

'You did great!' I said, and we laughed. 'You dug your dog's grave.'

We planted the grave out with flowers.

You can't always know what you are preparing for.

~

When Jet died, a heaviness settled on my chest. I knew that my lover, of all people, understood the grief of losing a dog, but I didn't make any attempt to let him know. He was overseas, on another visit to his homeland. Initially, he'd made regular contact, more regular than on past trips. He'd chatted to me while walking in the mountains, telling me what food was available nearby, food that I might like, as though perhaps in the future I might accompany him. This had felt meaningful, that he was envisaging some kind of 'us'. My heart filled with hope. But, after a couple of weeks, the contact dwindled to nothing, and my hope faded. I felt aggrieved, heartsore, forgotten. In this low state, I couldn't tell him about my dog. Thinking of my lover, I always came back to the same sensation of undernourishment. Needing a certain amount of affection, contact, lovingness, and being underwhelmed to the point of sorrow. How could I nourish myself if my lover could not be relied upon to do so?

~

The September fire threat passed and I urged my mother to go on a long-planned holiday. But, after she left, the fire threat flared again, with greater intensity. As the smoke got thicker and thicker and the Rural Fire Service warnings more dire, I listened to local ABC radio updates around the clock and endlessly pressed refresh on the Fires Near Me app. I watched the line of the fire inch closer and closer on the screen, only national park between us and the fire front. Milla and his girlfriend had also flown overseas. That left me, Luca and his girlfriend with the pets, the household objects and the decisions. My brother was watching the Fires Near Me app from his city. My mother was watching the app from Japan. They were both terrified. My ninety-eight-year-old nanna called from her city, sobbing. I told her I would get out early. I didn't tell her that I had no idea when 'early' would be.

My phone started beeping incessantly with new Fires Near

Me app notifications. I'd set my 'watch zone' at a twenty-five-kilometre radius from my homeplace. Towns along from me, in multiple directions, were being evacuated. Was this early? On Sunday the warnings ramped up. Tuesday would be a horror day. Searing summer temperatures, wild winds. If the wind was a southerly, we were done for, and the wind was predicted to be a southerly.

We needed to be out by Tuesday. Early.

Luca and his girlfriend helped me load all my father's artworks into the car. We laid the frames flat, with towels and blankets in between the glass. I gathered all the photo albums, of which there were many. Nothing was digitised. There were so many objects in the house — how could we know what we would miss if it was to burn? The house itself was the precious thing; the contents had no real meaning. On Monday, I gathered knick-knacks and clothes and books and my mother's long skirts and her jewellery, none of which she had requested, but which, unexpectedly, were the only things I cared about. I also packed my new shampoo and conditioner, even though I knew it was available at the supermarket. After days of anxiety, I'd lost the ability to make rational decisions. On Monday afternoon, I messaged the father of my sons and told him I was evacuating to his house the next day.

'Really?' he messaged back. 'Is that necessary?'

He lived in a shiny new house on the coast. He had three spare bedrooms and no pets. In my mind at least, he owed me.

~

On Tuesday morning, the smoke wasn't much worse than the day before. Was now 'early' or was it still too early? From inside the forest, we had no perspective on the surrounding fires, only the constant beeping alerts from the Fires Near Me app, the encroaching fireline on the digital map, and the relentless 'we may not be able to help you' messages on the local radio.

'Are you out yet?' a friend in Tasmania emailed.

'I am having trouble deciding when is "early" enough,' I wrote back.

'Being too early is better than being too late,' was her instant reply.

For some reason, I needed to be told this by someone two thousand kilometres away, who was not my terrified mother or brother or nanna.

Luca was at work, but his girlfriend and her friend were at home to help me with the final packing. I took the wheelie bins up to the road: if our homeplace didn't burn to the ground, the rubbish would need to be collected. On the way up the driveway, I gazed at tree trunks I'd walked by all my life and imagined a world without them.

'I'm sorry,' I whispered. 'I'm so sorry.'

All those trees. My forest, my family. Strong, steadfast. I was abandoning them. I didn't know how to say goodbye. I stopped a second with the wheelie bin, stifling a sob. The wind picked up, caressing my face, the leaves whispering around me. It was smoky, but I could see a kookaburra perched in the branch above. The bird stared down at me. I laid my head on the wheelie bin and cried.

Back at the house, we caught the cats and loaded the catboxes into Luca's girlfriend's car. They started up yowling and I was glad I wouldn't be driving them. I watched the girls drive off and then I lined up all the hoses in visible places in the walkway so that if anyone came to defend my house, they would be able to find them. I gathered the last bits and pieces and motioned to the pup, and, though he had rarely left the forest, he jumped straight in the car.

How do you say goodbye to everything you've ever loved?

You close the car door and you drive.

~

My ex was at work, so I let myself in. After the forest, his house was a frightening moonscape, every interior surface shiny and white. The pup raced inside, but balked at the polished cement floor. He held his paws up, one at a time, looking around him in shock. A quick U-turn later, he was back out the door, desperate and frightened, scratching at the car to get back in.

'It's too hot in the car,' I said, bending down to pat him. He stopped scratching and stared into my eyes. My mother was the matriarch, but she was not here. I was second in command. 'You have to come inside,' I pleaded.

He turned to follow me.

The girls had arrived before me, and they helped me put the bewildered cats in the laundry.

'They cried the whole way here,' Luca's girlfriend said. I could tell it had been excruciating. 'I didn't know cats did that. Cried like babies.'

The cats eyed me from the back of their catboxes. Sullen. I was their torturer. They wouldn't come out.

~

The day I evacuated, my lover finally called. He was home and catching up on the fire news.

'Just ringing to check you're holding up.' Such lightness in his tone. 'What with this dreaded fire business.'

It wasn't even a question. Of course I'd be holding up, his tone seemed to imply. Those bothersome fires! He had no idea how close the fires were to my homeplace, or that I'd packed up my belongings, piled them into a car and fled to my ex's. He hadn't asked and I hadn't told him.

I cried down the line, overcome.

'Oh, and I made a joke,' he said sadly. 'I made a joke when it is serious.'

~

When my ex got home from work, he made us dinner. Whatever resistance he'd had to my arrival had fallen away. In another life we'd been mother and father. We shared children, those giants, and it was odd, after all this time, to find ourselves awkward strangers. Luca and his girlfriend fled to a friend's house down the road, as though the prospect of watching the two of us struggle to interact was too much to bear, on top of everything else. My ex and I made polite chit-chat over dinner. His food was, as always, exceptionally good. When he left the next morning, I ate all his chocolate. No doubt, he knew I would.

~

Our world was dying. But the part of our brain that liked to sweat the small stuff couldn't be overridden. We tried. We learned to meditate. We poured money into self-improvement, hoping if we could just get steady enough in our thinking, in ourselves, we could put all these frivolous things aside and concentrate on the challenge ahead, but we couldn't. We couldn't stay off Facebook or stop scrolling through Instagram or constantly checking for an engaging email. We couldn't hold the enormity of the dying earth in our minds for any period of time. We were perpetually distracted. It was soothing to worry about kids and pets and money and sex. The big things had become little things, but we pretended not to see. It's what I did, obsessing day to day about my lover, while my homeplace, the love of my life, was dying. The drought was killing the garden. Perhaps in my lifetime the forest would be gone, unable to sustain the life that had once thrived there. My home had been a place of safety, inside a blessed circle, and now it wasn't. Maybe in the apocalypse there was no blessed circle?

Our collective inability to take action on anything about climate change seemed like laziness, or selfishness, or apathy, but as the fires roared towards my homeplace, it suddenly felt much more sinister. Was it now a form of collective suicide? Not only could we not save ourselves and our world, we were actively destroying it. We were like addicts unwilling to stop while our lives crumbled around us. Our children marched in protest on the streets, but still we carried on. What was driving our collective impulse towards annihilation?

On Tuesday, the wind did not blow from the south. It changed direction and blew over the hill instead, into the next town. Houses were lost there, but only a few. We were lucky and they were not. It did not seem like a cause for celebration. Back home in the forest, in the crackling dry, our trees were still dying. The fire was still burning in the national park behind our place, uncontainable. I went home but I didn't unpack the car. Another change in wind direction, another southerly, and I'd be ready to run. Adrenaline constantly surged through my body. I spent the days moving hoses, trying to save the dying trees. The creek was still trickling. If it dried up, the garden was finished. The world outside the forest was turning a deep brown. All around us ancient trees stood dead in the paddocks. Desolation everywhere.

The fires around our place had started in September, and reached their peak in November. Two months of constant flight or fight. I scarcely left home for fear that, if the wind changed direction, I wouldn't have time to rescue my pets. Even when I left to buy groceries, I felt panicked. What if I never saw my home again? What if I didn't get to say goodbye? At some point during that fraught time, Nika coaxed me down to the coast for a swim. I could no longer swim at home after the waterhole was destroyed in the floods. We met halfway between our respective homes in the hills, where a tidal river ran through the centre of town to meet up with the sea. At high tide, the river was clear and aquamarine, whereas at low tide it was gunky and brown. The summer before the fires, Nika and I had met up every second day or so to get our fill of the cooling water, timing it as best as we could for the high tides. That day, Nika called and said, 'It's high tide. Meet me at the river.' Although we were both frightened of leaving home, we did.

At our special spot, sheltered by overhanging casuarinas, we stripped off and hung our towels over the feathery branches. I was jittery, that heart-thumping anxiety of leaving home rising up. In the water, it was better. Calmer. We bounced around, chatting. It felt strange to be frolicking during the apocalypse. The world had changed, but the river was still there, with all its shimmering beauty.

'I'm just going to check my phone,' I said, suddenly anxious again.

I got out and poked around in my bag for the phone, then wiped the screen clean with the edge of my towel.

Three messages. I only read the first one: 'Better get home, Jess. The wind's changed.' Fear tore through me. Wet and dripping, I ran to the car and drove.

It was a false alarm, in that with the wind change the fire burnt someone else's house not ours, but I was overwhelmed by remorse for my lack of vigilance. I'd gone to the river. I'd been beguiled by its normalcy. I'd swum, dunking my head beneath the water. A momentary lapse in my attention. At home, I started pacing the periphery of our property again, refreshing the app.

Keep guard! my body screamed. Do not, for one second, look away!

~

'I'm thinking of coming home early,' my mother messaged from Japan. 'All I do over here is worry.'

I wanted to tell her I had it under control. Milla and his girlfriend would be home soon. There'd be more of us to carry the load.

'I would like that,' I typed instead. 'I don't know how long I can do this.'

It took three days to organise flights.

My mother messaged me from Tokyo airport, 'I'll be on the plane in two hours.'

Minutes later, it was raining. A wall of water, a thunderous roar.

I lay on the couch and listened, willing the rain to continue.

Drench us, I begged. Fucking drench us.

~

A week after my mother returned, a wompoo pigeon crashed into the glass door of my canopy bedroom. The whole house shuddered, but we assumed it was a giant palm frond falling on the roof and didn't investigate. Later, I found the bird dead on my doorstep. My mother adored wompoos. Bright like rainbow lorikeets, but large and round, their call was low and strange. *Wom-poo*, like an owl or a frog. When we caught sight of them in the trees, we watched them with delight. Wompoo pigeons were rare and spectacular. They were also clumsy and loud, rambunctious, hanging from trees, as if they might tumble out. They often built spindly nests over the creek, a precarious place to procreate. As far as we knew, they lived in pairs. Now one was dead, we couldn't stop thinking of its mate. We were killers. Erecting our glass doors in birds' flight paths. Fooling them with our vast reflected forests. My mother cradled the dead wompoo like a baby. We trudged around the house, my mother in front, me following, showing the spectacular body to the children, who were now adults. The world was upside down. We no longer knew how to cry.

After more rain, the fire threat dissipated. The fire in the national park behind our home was finally deemed 'under control'. I asked my lover to visit, and he surprised me by accepting my invitation.

'You look exactly the same,' I said, when I picked him up from the airport, as though it had been one hundred years and I'd expected him to be ancient.

'So do you,' he said, and we studied each other.

At some point during the fires, I'd hurt my leg and was trying not to limp.

My lover said nothing about my limp, though I knew he would have noticed it. Refraining from noting imperfections or weaknesses was his version of politeness.

'I pulled a muscle,' I said, by way of explanation, although I had no idea why my leg was so painful and had made no attempt to go to the physio to find out. How typical! I thought. This man twenty years older than me looks so sprightly, while I hobble along, fire-weary and injured. Everything about me, as always, on display.

My lover only stayed a few days, but seemed pleased by my efforts to be hospitable. I was pleased he was pleased, but more than anything I was exhausted. The fire was over, but the after-effects were still reverberating. While attempting to entertain my lover, dragging myself around with a conspicuous limp, I knew the end of the fires was only a seasonal reprieve. What about next summer? How could we defend our undefendable forest homeplace from the next hottest, driest summer on record?

~

'You stopped visiting as often,' my lover said, on the final night of his stay. We lay side by side on my bed, quiet in the stultifying summer heat. 'I thought … maybe this won't be a thing.'

He sounded dejected. I remembered the deal I'd made, the test I'd put him through and how he'd failed it. You never initiated a visit! I wanted to say. But I didn't. What if I had been brave enough, in that time of great anxiety, to just ask for reassurance?

'It's something, don't you think,' I said instead, turning towards him, 'that all this time there's never been anybody else but you?'

He looked surprised, as if this was a revelation. Had he imagined there'd been others?

'If there ever is,' he said, glancing away from me, 'I don't want to know a thing about it.'

I was surprised now — this seemed a new level of avoidance.

'Well, I don't feel like that,' I said. 'I'd definitely want to know.'

~

A couple of months later, I organised another trip to his city. Before I arrived, I fantasised about fucking, but mostly I fantasised about lying on his comfortable couch, reading books, responsible for nothing and no one. I let myself in while he was at work and looked around his neat home. Flower arrangements, my fluffy towel, the books laid out on the bed, the fresh bread. I sighed with pleasure.

When I'd left home that morning, the skies looked ominous. Flooding was predicted. After the stress of losing the little house, it was easy to forget that flooding was normal in northern New South Wales, that it usually happened once or twice a year. This time the local news predictions sounded catastrophic, but I was trying to remain calm.

I chose a book from my lover's selection and settled on the couch to read. When he came home, that's where he found me, curled up with a book, creating my imprint on his ordinarily imprint-less white couch.

He seemed the same as always: warm, congenial, but with a vague unknowable quality. Just the way I liked him. He made dinner and we ate, and then we read, separate but together, in his lounge room. When reading, he never sat close to me on the couch. I would have liked to snuggle a little as we read, but this was not his way. In the beginning I occasionally approached him, tried to sit close, inhabit the same space, but he had always seemed uncomfortable, so I'd learned to stay on my own side. But even that compromise felt peaceful the first night of this visit. I wasn't anxious anymore. Let him have his own space. Didn't I like my own space too? Isn't that why I was there?

While we were reading, my mother called. She rarely called

when I was staying at my lover's, so I knew it was serious. She said that it was flooding. We hadn't lost any part of our home, but the water was gushing in a torrent along the walkway, right down the centre of the house. That had never happened before. The water had risen so high, it had seeped inside the walls and flooded the interior of the lounge room.

She sounded frazzled. What a big, wet mess it all was. I knew what that kind of flooding would feel like, and I'd never been more relieved not to be at home. My mother had missed most of the bushfires — let her manage this flood without me.

My lover listened to my end of the phone call.

'It's very different up there,' he said, when I finally hung up.

That was an understatement.

'We seem to be experiencing the effects of climate change in a way that hasn't reached the city yet,' I said, feeling faintly defensive. I'd always believed that my homeplace would somehow be the last place to feel the effects of climate change. The wettest. The greenest. The safest. It was a shock to realise this wasn't true. It now seemed as if my homeplace was at the epicentre of this new turbulent weather.

'It feels very real up there,' I said.

He was silent, watching me.

'It doesn't feel like that here, does it?' I was envious. How I longed for that obliviousness.

'No,' he agreed. 'It doesn't.'

~

Something felt different between us this time — looser, easier, settled. When we fucked, there was more talking. I felt safer, more open. I wanted him in different ways, with less restraint, and I was willing to say so. We fucked on the couch. We fucked on the floor of his bedroom.

It's not very comfortable here,' he said halfway through, and I laughed. He was right.

'Shall we get into bed?'

I scrambled up, knocking my hip, as usual, on his bedpost as I bumped past. It would bruise, I knew from experience. Some things never changed. In the centre of his bed, we knelt together, naked and open, watching each other's faces. I reached out and slid my forearm against his chest. He looked at me and nodded.

This is us, he seemed to say.

On the Sunday, we went into the city to see an art exhibition, and we paid for the guided tour. The gallery attendant gave us each big cushiony wireless earphones that were relatively sound-cancelling, so when the guide paused between artworks, the crowded gallery seemed utterly silent. Disorientated, I almost collided with the people around me. I kept an eye on my lover and he kept an eye on me, but I stuck to the unspoken rule of our public life: not standing too close, giving no perceptible sign that there was anything of the couple about us.

I looked at the paintings, glad of the guided tour. Without it, I would have been lost. The older man loved to go to galleries, but I always felt at sea. Visual art was a language I couldn't comprehend. I made myself stare at the artwork, but I was always more drawn to the captions.

I felt my lover then, behind me. Closer than I expected. I glanced back and smiled, and he leaned his body gently against mine. He exerted no pressure, but I felt the length of him along my back. It was so unlike him, this public touch, that I was startled. Recovering, I leaned back into his frame. He placed his fist inside the curve of my hand and I cupped his fingers in mine. It was the smallest gesture, the lightest embrace, but I teared up with the intimacy.

He loves me, I thought. This is love.

~

My lover liked to check the weather. This trip he said, 'What's it like at your house?'

He showed me his screen: he had his phone set so that when he checked his weather, my weather came up too. I wondered how long he'd been doing that. Perhaps since the fires? Tracking the weather in my life. All these small ways to feel connected.

~

That first weekend of my trip I was high. It was flooding at home, but it wasn't my problem. I was in the city with my lover, being loved.

He went back to work on Monday and, once he was gone, I became teary. The weekend high had given way to a sudden feral vulnerability. He deserved someone better than me. He deserved someone *available*, not someone who lived two thousand kilometres away. He had been kind and loving and soft and open, and in response I was a tearful, frightened mess.

You are having a reaction, I told myself sternly. You are having a reaction to feeling loved.

I caught a tram into the city to get some pho, which I found soothing. And perhaps getting out of the house would help. My eyes welled up intermittently on the tram, but I hoped my sunglasses hid my tears.

Chinatown was oddly empty. Is it that virus? I thought, looking around. Racists steering clear of Chinese restaurants? Surely not! I'd heard about the virus on the news but, thus far, it was only in China, they said. A distant threat.

I went to the same restaurant I always went to. Plastic tabletops under hideous fluoro lighting, but with the yummiest pho. The restaurant was usually packed, noisy patrons pressed together, the staff harried. This time there were only three or four customers.

I sat down and the waiter came to take my order.

While I waited for my pho, I started crying again, surreptitiously dabbing my eyes with a napkin. A man seated across the way was watching me, as if he was about to offer some comforting words, but I avoided his gaze.

I texted Nika instead.

SOS. Can't stop crying at pho place.

It's so weird, I only feel safe or worthy if he keeps me at a distance.

I feel like I've forced him into being with me. He's finally given up fighting it, so now I'm preventing him from being with someone who: a. he could truly be happy with, and b. someone better and nicer than me.

I suddenly feel really guilty about it.

I was on a roll, I couldn't stop.

Why am I throwing up reasons to be unloved? Like an avoidant at work? Am I trying to find an excuse to leave him?

Why is this my response to being treated more lovingly?

I feel so undeserving.

When he treats me like his heart isn't in it, I don't have to worry so much about whether I am actually good for him.

My pho came and I mixed in the mint and added the chilli. I was still dripping tears, but I wiped them away, nonchalantly, with my napkin. I glanced at the man across from me. He appeared poised to come to my aid, but I tried my best to look as if I'd pulled myself together.

I continued texting Nika:

He'll probably turn cold on me at some stage, like he always does. And then I can go back to feeling more comfortable.

I picked up some noodles with my chopsticks, sucking the soft white strands into my mouth, tears trickling down my face.

I'm literally crying into my pho. Laughing, crying emoji.

The chilli in the pho made my nose run more than the tears had, and I quietly blew into a napkin.

I felt the man across from me still watching my face. I looked up at him and smiled.

I've got this. Nothing to see here.

I rode out my uncomfortable feelings. When my lover came home in the evenings, I kept the emotion of the day to myself. He didn't seem to notice. As predicted, in the days that followed, my lover reverted to his ordinary behaviour. Occasional bouts of remoteness followed by warmth and amiability, followed by a slight withdrawal of affection, and repeat. It was anxiety-provoking, but in the way I was used to. Anyway, hadn't I known the frightening love-feeling wouldn't last?

On the second-last morning of my trip, we sat across from each other at his kitchen table, eating breakfast.

'Look at the way you're sitting,' he said.

'What?' I looked up, surprised at his tone of voice.

He slouched to the side, demonstrating my messy sprawl.

'I mean, you complain about being in pain, but you don't even try to sit up straight.' He sounded genuinely irritated.

I stared at him across the table. It was true that my posture was sloppy, but he had never criticised anything about me.

'You could do exercises, you know, to help.'

'You're right,' I said mildly. 'I should.'

What was that? I thought. Was there now enough familiarity between us for him to nag me like an exasperated schoolmaster? Or was he trying to pick a fight? It would take more than that to rile me. But I took note.

~

That afternoon, I met up with my brother for a drink. He asked me how it had been with my lover.

'A bit of a roller coaster,' I said, and heard myself sigh.

I explained how loved he had made me feel at the beginning of the trip, how I'd had a weird bout of crying, and how my lover had switched to sudden left-of-field critique.

'Maybe it's a sign that he feels more comfortable with me,' I suggested hopefully. 'But he sounded like a cranky old man.'

'Yeah, I don't know,' my brother said. He always withheld judgement. He was the kindest man I knew.

I scanned my brother's face for any fleeting sense of concern. Was he worried? Should I be worried?

'I mean, it's okay. It's not like he hurt my feelings that much. It's just, he's never treated me like that before.'

'Some people take criticism simply as feedback,' my brother said.

'Imagine being like that?' I laughed, and he laughed. Criticism as feedback was not part of our family culture.

'It was fine,' I said, 'but I don't know if I'd cope if he did it too often.'

Was I demarcating a boundary about behaviour I wouldn't tolerate in future? Boundaries were so antithetical to how I'd been raised, they always felt oddly experimental. I was feeling my way in.

~

That night, lying in bed with my lover, some of my crying-over-pho feelings rose up.

He was reading, but I interrupted.

'Sometimes I feel bad that, because of me, you don't have someone down here,' I said, forcing the words out.

He looked across at me, calm, unruffled.

'Jessie, you don't need to think about that,' he said, taking off his glasses. 'We are together. I'm with you now.'

He had never said something so reassuring. Just like that, as though it was nothing. I had longed for a sense of ongoingness, this affirmation, but I had given up on it ever being verbalised.

I was thrown — excited, terrified — my body started to shake. I hoped it didn't show.

'Okay,' I said, trying to recalibrate. 'Okay.'

~

I was flying home the next morning. In preparation, I scurried around trying to gather my things. I'd used all the willpower I could muster to keep my belongings neatly in one place, but I'd still failed. There were also additional items that no longer fitted in my tiny bag.

'I'll just leave this here, if that's okay,' I said, pointing to an offending object.

'Why don't you take it with you?' he said.

'I can just get it next time I come,' I said.

He nodded, but I saw a frown flicker across his face.

Even now he doesn't want to commit to a next time, I thought. Back to that dance.

I sighed, and he hugged me goodbye, and I took my roller bag out onto the footpath to catch a tram to the airport bus.

Ten minutes before I boarded, he called, as was his custom.

'Have a safe trip,' he said. 'Take care.'

~

On arrival, I had a message from Nika, checking in on how I'd adjusted after the pho crying.

Well, one thing's for certain.

We are together. Love heart emoji.

The only way is through.

~

Back home, I started planting. After the flood, I'd requisitioned a sunny, open spot, near where the little house had stood, to start a flower garden. It was a way to rebuild, and flowers, of all descriptions, were a joy. Their bright faces, titling towards the light. The seasonal nature of their blooming. The waiting and waiting for the buds to appear. The surprise when they did. We always had a mass of spectacular bromeliads in our forest, but there was so much green it was hard for them to compete, and I longed for a spectrum of colour. Before the flood, I'd never been a gardener. I had few skills, but I knew what I liked, and now the flower garden was blooming around me.

—

A week after returning home, I had three missed calls from my lover, which always gave me a tingle of alarm. But as I kept my phone on silent, I often missed calls. When I called back, he sounded so stricken, so strange, that my first thought was, oh god — cancer — it's terminal.

He wanted to go through the motions of small talk, but I could only hear the awful wrongness in his voice.

'Just tell me what it is,' I said. 'What's happened?'

I was thinking that he'd lost his job. That there had been an accident. I was thinking someone he loved had died.

'I think we need to stop,' he said.

Even though I didn't see these words coming, I knew exactly what he meant. He didn't say 'break up' or 'end', because what we had was never defined in those terms. There was nothing to break and nothing to end, just a pattern of behaviour that had to stop.

'Um,' I said. 'Um.'

Just like that, I was disembodied, empty space all around me.

He elaborated. 'Look, with you up there and me down here, I don't really have a life. I meet a lot of people, but because of our—' He stopped dead, grappling again with the terminology.

Our situation, I thought. Relationship? Involvement?

I said nothing.

'I've met someone,' he blurted out. Starting the conversation again. Starting at the truthful spot.

I was floating. Still mute.

'Someone I think I could really feel something for.'

It had to stop, I thought. Whatever we were doing had to stop.

The emptiness around me expanded. I was sitting alone in my study, but the study had disappeared. I was like an astronaut, the phone my oxygen cord, my lifeline, stopping me from pinging off into oblivion. In this empty space, numerous things were suddenly clear. The constancy of his half-heartedness. How I'd chosen it again and again. How he was really no different from any of the others. How foolish I'd been. How little he cared for me.

Inside me, dread was rising. I was overcome with sudden nausea. I couldn't feel anything but the sick-belly-rolling.

She was older, he admitted. His voice was strangely light, almost gleeful, as if with every word he spoke he was regaining self-respect. Had he always been ashamed of desiring me?

'I've never been in love with you,' he said. 'I thought you knew that.'

'No,' I shook my head. I hadn't believed it.

'We had that conversation,' he said.

I'd spent so much time anxious about my lover's feelings — analysing, weighing things up — but I hadn't truly absorbed that conversation. That was one time, I wanted to say. One time. All the other moments I had catalogued to balance out that one conversation rushed towards me.

'I feel sick,' I whispered. A cold sweat broke out across my forehead and my cheeks. I put my head between my knees. What had started as an experiment with desire, with uncertainty, had — for me — become so much more.

'Just sit with me for a while,' I said. 'Don't hurry off.'

If he stayed on the phone it didn't have to stop. I wanted to have a response, something I might report to him, but I had nothing.

We were silent together.

'I don't know what else to say,' he said finally.

'Please check in with me.' It was all I could muster.

Already, I was drowning in fear about how hard I would take this. What I'd feel when the sick numbness ended. It had not occurred to me that he might develop feelings for someone else. Feelings strong enough to act on, strong enough to put a stop to what we had. I'd become so immune to his half-heartedness, I'd come to see it as part of who he was, not directed at me, not personal. But it was personal. And now we had to stop.

'I don't care about the sex part,' I finally said. 'I just care about the other stuff.'

What I was trying to say was — don't cut me off suddenly. Cutting me off suddenly will really fuck me up. I thought about my father. I thought about the eight-hour plane trip after the phone call to say that he was dead. That same nothingness. All that empty space.

'It's just, the way my dad left me, it's much worse if you cut me off.'

I thought about how I'd often lain face-down along the length of my lover's body, after we'd fucked. Resting there, merging, feeling his heartbeat against my chest.

'I will call,' he said softly. 'I will call you on the weekend.'

'Not just on the weekend,' I said. 'Call me for months.'

I knew how long it would take. I said months, but I meant years.

'And you can check on me.' He said it lightly, as though the call had gone better than expected.

Silence again.

'Um, okay.' I said finally. 'Okay.'

'Okay?' I could sense his relief. He sounded elated.

~

'He's set me free,' I said when I cried to my mother. She watched me, her face full of knowing. Nothing at all anymore a surprise.

~

The next night, still dumbstruck, I drove to the cinema forty minutes away to watch a movie — a distraction. Afterwards, my car wouldn't start. I called the NRMA, but it had to be towed. Luca and his girlfriend came to pick me up.

It was dark inside the capsule of my son's car and I cried silently in the back seat.

'He broke up with me,' I piped up after a few minutes. My

shame was ballooning. Why didn't adulthood mean you got smarter?

Luca and his girlfriend shifted in their seats, glancing across at each other.

'The long-distance thing no good?' Luca asked finally.

'I guess so,' I said, my voice trembling. 'I guess that's what it was.'

My son turned on the radio. Now I had cover for my crying. He and his girlfriend bickered gently about each song that came on. It was a strange reversal. My child was now the driver and I was in the back seat, sitting there with all my bad choices, crying into the sleeves of my jumper.

When we got home and we all headed off to bed, a message popped up from Luca: 'Mum, I love you.'

~

And then there was the weekend call, when I was not so mute with shock. For the older man, the connection between us had been severed. The weekend call was just the after-work. Going through the motions of doing right by someone. I heard it in his voice. Talking to me was already a drag.

I was still quiet, but I could ask a question or two.

It turned out that he already had a date planned with the new person when I was down there. He had now been on the date. Which meant that, when I was visiting, he knew it was over between us. It was only me who was out of the loop. I flipped back through the twelve days of my visit, seeking out the signs I'd missed. They existed, no doubt, but I was caught by the memory of his cock in my hand, his semen sprayed all over my belly. All the sex we had in the twelve days when he knew and I didn't.

How open I was, how trusting.

How oblivious.

The way he talked during the weekend call, it was as if everything should have been clear to me. Why, he asked, would I ever have assumed there was anything involving deep feeling between us?

Not in love was one thing, nothing involving deep feeling was another.

How different our two narratives were!

I had believed the love he had for me was all the love he was capable of. He had believed he could not love me, but could love someone new.

And still, in my mind, the flashes of his cock and all the ways it was inside me. He said he didn't know what he could have done differently. Inside my mouth. He said he never meant for this to happen. Inside my arse. He said he didn't see it coming. Inside my cunt. The way my lover spoke, it was as though he had tripped on something in the dark. This other woman. Completely accidental.

'It would have been better if we'd only slept together that first night,' he said. He said it more than once.

He wished everything that came after was erased.

Four years of my life.

He wished it away.

I was an inconvenience. A regret.

I slid off the couch in the study onto the floor. I placed my forehead on the carpet. I curled up in child's pose.

'I just want an ordinary life!' he said bitterly. 'An. Ordinary. Life.'

It was so much worse than I expected.

~

Our relationship had grown so big in my mind and remained so small in his. It was my habit to grow things, his habit to cut things back. He was concise, clipped, self-discipline always one of his most appealing traits. He'd kept the idea of me small. Any imaginings that shot up, reaching for the sky, he cut back, perhaps even poisoned. In his house in the city he had a tiny garden, always tended. There was a passionfruit vine growing on his back fence, wild and unruly. He often talked of cutting it back, of replacing it with something less invasive, less messy. 'It shits me,' he'd say. It had taken me some time to realise this passionfruit vine was me.

~

I have been so wildly alone in all this. I have been alone the whole time.

~

I called Lou, and she said, 'Come up! Just get in the car and come up!' It was all there in her voice: agitation, fear, concern. I heard her explaining things to her husband.

'Mike says, just come now,' she said emphatically. 'Please come! We love you!'

I knew Lou would see all the parallels with the death of my father. The shock of being left, so little warning. A decision made without me, enacted from afar. The destruction of trust. This new loss ricocheted backwards through time, rekindling the devastation of all that earlier grief. I pictured Lou's house, two hours' drive away, so welcoming, so peaceful. I wanted to see her, to be held, but I couldn't get out of child's pose. Perhaps I was holding myself?

~

All my anxiety — my obsessive fear of abandonment — had not prepared me. Did watching a bushfire in the distance, knowing it might come your way, mean it hurt less if your house was lost? Grief, it seemed, was not alleviated by the awareness of risk.

~

I was a stone thrown into a deep creek. I was dropping down down down. A slow tumble through dark water. I didn't fight it. Bubbles streamed around me. Resistance was futile. I curled into the foetal position. Let me be streamlined, I thought. Let's get it over with. The fall couldn't be stopped. I hadn't hit the bottom yet, but I knew it was coming. I was braced, waiting for the crash.

~

Every day after the weekend call I swam laps at the pool. I cry-gulped my way along the lanes, my goggles filling with tears. The rhythmic nature of pool-crying was soothing. The tears didn't start straightaway, I swam the first few laps like an ordinary person, but then the emotion engulfed me like a wave. Chest-heaving sobbing, no slow build. It could last for many laps. The longer it lasted, the better I felt afterwards. Then one day, the sobbing didn't come. I teared up as I parked my car, and thought, I'm just in time. But in the pool nothing happened. Without tears, I was bereft.

~

This is not the book I want to be writing.

~

A sudden bout of red-raw acne sprung up on my left cheek. I had often experienced mild breakouts, but never anything like this. My cheek was angry, my cheek was aflame. Every morning I turned my face to examine the bizarre eruption in the bathroom mirror. Okay, face, I thought. Let it all hang out. You are in pain. This is the rage. Display it!

~

Retaining hope used to be a matter of — well, look, the birds still sing, the crickets chirp, the purple flowering tree still blossoms. But now, we spin towards the apocalypse, and it is more like — well, *today* the birds are singing, the crickets are chirping, the purple flowers are blooming, but the promise of forever, of safety, has vanished. Close your eyes and everything you love is gone.

~

Early one morning, Milla came into the kitchen before work. I was standing at the stove, waiting for the kettle to boil, listening to the swish and click of the forest.

'Mum?' he said, glancing at my inflamed cheek. 'You okay?'

I hadn't told him about the older man's decision, but it seemed he knew.

I shrugged. My fiery cheek was speaking for me.

Milla came closer, holding out his arms for a hug. I stepped into his embrace. He towered above me, my giant child. I laid my cheek against his chest. He held me there, the seconds ticking by. For a big man, he had the lightest touch.

~

I told Nika that my lover claimed he just wanted an ordinary life. Not missing a beat, she quipped, 'You are too extraordinary for him!' I smiled, but thought, extraordinary can mean many things. Would I never be ordinary in a way that was lovable, stayable, chooseable, right?

~

My phone rang, an unknown number. Usually, I ignored them but this time, in the fugue of despair, I answered.

'Look, I've got your cat. I'm real sorry, but he's looking bad.' I recognised the voice straightaway. That first man I'd loved after breaking up with the father of my kids. The wildman, so spectacularly wrong for me. So alluring, but far too direct. The man from my novel. Why did he have my cat?

'What's going on?' I asked, bewildered.

'Look, I've got your cat. I found him on the road and I saw he had a name tag. I'm sorry, but he's not looking good. You wanna come and get him?'

Only William's name and our number were on his tag. I realised that my old flame didn't know he'd called me. He didn't know it was my cat.

'It's me,' I said. 'It's Jessie.'

'Jessie?' he laughed. 'Fark. How are ya?'

Shattered, I wanted to say.

'Yeah, alright,' I said. 'So, you've got William? Where are you? I'll come and get him.'

I hadn't set eyes on this man for years. I used to be unsettled by even a sighting of his car. Whatever it was we'd shared happened at least a decade ago. Him popping up now, in such an improbable way, instantly felt like some kind of cosmic sign. Shut up, I said to that part of my brain. Just stop.

'I live down the road now, been here about a year,' he said. 'I'll bring him round.'

He had lived a few towns away when I'd known him. I couldn't believe he was now my neighbour. Why had I never seen him?

Five minutes later, he pulled up outside. It was not the ute I remembered. He got out and I stared at him, my body aquiver. It felt as though my skin was shimmering with grief, but I didn't know if it was visible. My acned left cheek was surely speaking vibrantly of my suffering.

He was the same as he'd always been. Handsome devil. Those dark, curved lashes, that direct stare. Right then, I wanted to sit in his lap.

My mother came out to the driveway to greet him.

'Look, I don't think the cat's gonna make it,' he said to us, opening the back door of his car. William was wrapped in a towel on the backseat, staring vacantly into space. I could only glance at him, already at my limit of coping.

'I don't think he's been hit,' my old flame continued. 'Must be poison, or a snakebite.'

'Mum, you'll have to pick him up,' I said. 'I can't.'

My mother gathered William up carefully, cradling him in

the dirty towel.

'Oh, William,' she crooned, staring down at him. He had always been her favourite. Independent, adventurous, capricious, difficult to feel loved by. Her kind of cat.

'I'm sorry,' my old flame said. 'He's too far gone. I didn't know if I should even call.'

'No. Thank you,' I said. 'We'll take him to the vet. He's very beloved.'

'Okay,' he said, moving back towards his car.

'Nice to see you,' I said, because it was. 'It's been a while.'

'Call me,' he said, direct as ever, and then he got back in the car and drove away.

—

It was a snakebite. Though the red-headed vet pumped William full of antivenom — for which we owed three thousand dollars — he still died. My mother was heartbroken. This time Milla dug the hole and buried William. My older son did not dry-retch. He must have inherited my strong stomach. We buried Jet and William, months apart, the two elders of our family. I remembered the way they had always loved each other so unambivalently. When I walked out to the car, I would often turn back for a last look, and they would be there, together in the walkway, watching me leave, sitting side by side, like statues, their tails intertwined.

—

Was it, in fact, meaningful that, in the week after a soul-crushing breakup, a man I once crazy-loved (enough to write a whole novel in his voice) found our half-dead cat on the road, called me without knowing it was me and then delivered the cat to my door? In other words, should I call him?

~

I called him and we met for a walk on the beach. He might have looked the same as he always had, but he had been through the wringer. Homelessness, hunger, isolation. I was astonished. This man had often skirted the edges, but I'd imagined him as endlessly resilient, always landing on his feet. But he had stumbled, fallen. As we walked along the beach, his need to be heard was so overwhelming I barely got a word in, and all the while I fought the urge to see his reappearance in my life as evidence of some kind of cosmic flow. I thought of how much I'd loved this man, and how much the woman who'd come before me had also loved him, and the woman who'd come after me too. Afterwards, it dawned on me that what I might glean from this sudden seren-dipitous reconnection (if gleaning, in this situation, was even a necessary thing) was that shunning love, year after year, left you deeply lonely. So much squandered love.

~

Between the crying jags and the blank-minded nothingness

and the black-bellied pain and the tight-chest stress, there were moments when I felt a sense of relief from the constant gnawing possibility that the older man might reject me. I was post-rejection. The worst had already happened.

~

In this strange heightened state, I started to suspect the weather was mimicking my internal landscape. Ever since the flood had destroyed the little house, rain had made me anxious, but now it was soothing, a reflection of how bad I felt. Of course, it's gloomy out there! Look how it is inside me! I knew, rationally, this belief was a form of grandiose thinking, but I felt it anyway. Every day my emotions cycled like the weather: broody dark skies, the sudden boom of thunder, unexpected sunshine laughter, and even the odd sunset high. Sometimes I woke in the morning and it wasn't all gloom and doom. Sometimes I woke in the night to a dream in which the older man was trying to tell me about her, my replacement, and his voice when he said her name — awed, lovestruck — sent a stabbing pain through my chest. I woke breathless, gasping, as if I'd been struck by lightning.

~

All the warning signs my body had thrown my way, that his ambivalence was unsafe, and I'd refused to heed them. I'd chosen, instead, to see myself as malfunctioning, my body as recalcitrant, unnecessarily triggered. I'd believed I needed to relearn how to trust others, when what I needed was to relearn how to trust myself.

~

In sharing these words, I was breaking the pact of intimacy. What happens between us stays between us. How to navigate this new territory in writing? We believe ourselves protected by notions of privacy, but are some of us more protected than others? I thought of all the times I'd been discouraged from speaking, of what I'd been speaking of. Hurt, woundedness, betrayal, loss. Who does privacy serve? In our circumstances, privacy seemed to afford him so much protection and me none. Hush, girl.

~

In the first weeks after the phone call, the thing that brought me the most pleasure was the idea of the older man's suffering. I hoped he was in distress. I hoped, once his relief faded, he felt shame over what he'd done. I hoped he had some sense of what it meant to be careless with someone. I hoped he could see he'd been careless with me.

'Coward!' one friend hissed, when I told her of his phone call. 'What a coward!'

'Reptile!' cried another. 'Does this man have any human feeling?'

I collected comments like this. I hung them around my neck and I jingled them like necklaces. The sound was soothing.

~

Two weeks after the weekend call, the older man's name flashed on my phone. The shock of it ran through my body, and suddenly I was crying. I put the phone face-down and ran out the kitchen door, down the walkway and up the stairs to my canopy bedroom. I crawled onto my bed and under the covers, even my head. I lay there in the darkness and cried and cried, my old terror of the phone combined with a new terror of what additional heart-rending things the older man might say. Once I calmed down, I went back downstairs. I assumed he was calling because I'd requested that he check in. I assumed that, once he'd tried to check in, he'd feel he'd done his duty. But he kept calling. Each time, I looked at the phone in horror, unable to answer it. Each time, I cried. After a few days, I became worried about him. I didn't want him to feel that I hated him, I was just terrified of the phone.

I texted, explaining. 'Can I write you a letter instead?'

'Of course,' he texted back. Of course.

~

I wrote a long letter, he wrote a short reply. I saw it had been an effort for him to get the words down. I was always too much and he was always too little. He admitted his manner of breaking off with me had been 'cack-handed', a word I had to google. An ideal adjective, it turned out. His use of it in that context wholly capturing him in a way I could never hope to. Humble, gentlemanly, borderline archaic.

~

When the first lockdown happened, it happened fast. I lived with the only people I saw regularly, so social distancing did not affect me much. But the pool closed, which put an end to any chance of the therapeutic pool-crying. Despite the lockdown, however, there was still grocery shopping, bushwalking, cooking, gardening, hanging out with my sons and their girls, chatting on the phone to Lou or Nika. All those parts of my normal life continued, while the world outside was irreconcilably changed.

~

The globe had begun spinning towards catastrophe, or an endless chain of catastrophes, and, still, we were expected to pin our hopes on the speedy return of our old lives. Buying and selling; hustling for livelihood. Capitalism. Neoliberalism. The very way of life that had created this exponential string of clusterfucks. Meanwhile, the rainforest burned. Meanwhile, we routinely evacuated our houses. Meanwhile, a deforestation-linked global pandemic pinned us in place.

What to do with the mountain of feeling that accumulated during a single day? I walked the lonely road outside my house, sometimes I even jogged, but the rhythmic sameness induced brooding rather than release. I started to walk the creek instead. Upstream, where it was unpeopled.

On my creek walks, all the details around me were heightened. Velvety fallen leaves, swooshing softly. Stray pine cones. Collapsed coral trees re-sprouting. Mushrooms covered in thick moss, growing up tree trunks like a stairway. And then there was the rubbish, the flood debris. Scraps of roofing tin. A broken folding chair. An electric powerboard, its cord hanging long behind it like a tail. Tufts of couch stuffing poking from between rocks. Chunks of rusting steel. Snakes of black plastic sheeting woven through the roots. Rags of green mesh caught high in the trees. The occasional glass bottle. The creek walk wasn't pristine; it was the whole messy catastrophe. Random, chaotic, ruinous, but still beautiful.

Walking the creek required a different kind of rhythm, each step unpredictable. There was no path amidst the giant boulders or tangled tree roots or impassable fallen logs. Sometimes I had to abandon the bank and clamber into the water. Into the deep was the only way through. I stepped along, watching my feet to figure out the best place to tread. Would I sink into that patch of mud? Was that boulder too slippery? Would I get caught up in those thorns? Sometimes I'd lose concentration and get overtaken by looping thoughts. Why doesn't he feel more for me? Why am I so forsaken? Before long, I was a crying girl again, tramping through the forest, forgetting to watch my step. The first time I took a tumble, I went down hard. I lost my balance on an unsteady rock, and landed in the rapids with a crash. I froze there, searing pain in my hands and knees, water rushing all around me. I lifted up one hand, and then the other. They were both bleeding. My knees were bleeding too. Why were rocks so hard! Why was everything so hard! I sat down in the shallows, weeping, shuddering, watching my hands and knees bleed. After a while, I looked downstream: the long view. Giant, graceful trees along the creek banks, leaves lit up in the filtered sunlight. A dazzling spaciousness. The breeze lifted, caressing my face. The leaves fell gently around me, like snowflakes. The truth was, rocks were only hard if you hit them with force. If you trailed your fingertips across them tenderly, they could be as smooth and soft as silk. I dipped my palms in the water, splashed my knees clean. As I stood up, I tested out my limbs. Everything worked fine. Walk on, I thought. Walk on.

~

After a month or so, I took the necklace of insults from around my neck. Its jingle no longer soothed me. The man I'd desired had his own reasons, his own repeating patterns. Closeness, withdrawal. Desire, betrayal. For a gracious man, he had been ungracious, but he had every right to seek an ordinary life. When

I thought of him now, I saw flashes of his frightened animal body, pink-skinned after a hot shower, covering his naked chest with a T-shirt when he caught my stare. Ageing before my eyes, unprotected. Not wanting to be seen.

~

After I told the older man I couldn't pick up, he stopped calling. Then, one morning, I woke feeling I'd washed up on a different shore. Something had shifted in my sleep. I could speak now. I could call. I reread his short letter. It seemed different from the way I'd first interpreted it. More heartfelt, more sorry. I thought back to my last visit to his city, to the reaction I'd had to feeling loved. Crying in my pho. Texting Nika SOS. How excruciating it had felt. The responsibility, the vulnerability. How hard I'd found it to ride out. What if the older man had a reaction too? What if he just hadn't ridden it out?

I knew my ability to call wouldn't last, so I dialled his number. He picked up before the first ring.

'Hello,' he said, his voice tight.

'Something's happened to me,' I said. 'I can call.'

'That's good,' he breathed out. 'How are you?'

It was an awkward, stifled exchange. The weather. The lockdown. His voice was like a closed door, almost unrecognisable. I wondered what the feeling was that he was locking away. The chat petered out. I pressed the phone to my ear, listening to the silence, trying to steady myself, trying to find the right question.

'How are you feeling about what happened between us?' Too direct perhaps, but it was all I had.

'It's regrettable,' he said after a few seconds, still that closed-door voice. 'I always do the wrong thing.'

'What do you mean?' I was checking myself, not jumping to any conclusions.

'Just, I always have,' he breathed out. 'I always do.'

He sounded like a man in mourning. Like he'd killed something precious. Those old patterns. His, this time, not mine. In hurting me, he has hurt himself, I thought. But was that true? Other people's inner worlds — so mysterious.

'What are you thinking?' I asked.

The longest pause.

'It was lovely,' he exhaled, his voice finally unlocking. 'All of it was lovely.'

An admission. Soft, full, warm.

I held my breath.

'But I think I still want to be with someone down here,' he sounded wistful. Lonely, even. 'A proper relationship.'

I didn't want to know about her. The other woman. I'd woken with fresh hope, as though my brain had somehow altered the narrative in my sleep, and now I was struggling to realign with reality.

'Really?' I thought of how much distance he'd needed to feel safe. How he'd believed the problem was me. But that it was also him.

He was quiet then.

'Yes, really.'

It seemed I needed to hear this again. I needed to believe it.

~

At night, during lockdown, my family gathered around the dinner table. My sons both worked in essential services, and they filled us in on what was happening in the outside world. The panic-buying, the everchanging restrictions. Our lives had become even more localised. The fullness of my family group swung into view. Six of us, the way it had been when I was a child. A small tribe. I looked around the table: my mother, my sons, the two girls. Illuminated, golden.

~

In this new world, post-bushfire, post-breakup, I found myself unexpectedly calm. My past history had taught me that my world could come undone at any moment. Even the most stable rug could be pulled. Though my body, with all its tics, was still displaying the effects of a nervous system on high alert, my mind during lockdown was becoming more elastic. I was bouncing back. Life should be like this, I thought. Restful, restorative, modest, slow. The acne on my left cheek subsided in the tranquillity.

~

On my creek walks, even when I was paying attention, a rock that felt steady could totter underfoot. Out of nowhere, I could be upended. On my hands and knees crying, bleeding in the same place I bled the first time. The landscape was constantly changing, always throwing up new surprises. Slippery moss that wasn't there yesterday, a fallen branch nudging a trusted stepping-stone to the right. Sometimes, if I was lucky, I'd retain my balance, wobbling there on that unsteady rock, but not every time. After a fall, I always sat quietly for a moment, taking it in. This stone. This air. This tree. The giant boulders all seemed distinct, but, walking the creek, I glimpsed them joined beneath the water. The floods had eroded the creek banks, leaving the tree roots exposed. A rare cross-section glimpse of the strata. Above the surface, the trees looked separate, but beneath the ground their roots were tangled in a wild network of together-ness, living and decaying, vast and complex. The rocks and trees weren't all separate entities, the rocks and trees were *the land*. I sat still, watching, my blood flowing with the water.

~

I drove to the beach to walk with Nika — 1.5 metres apart. It was busier than an ordinary pre-pandemic day, which disturbed me. I'd developed a touch of agoraphobia from staying home for too long. I'd experienced it before. The world outside my homeplace seemed surreal; my perception was heightened. Colours were brighter, sounds louder. My body moved more jerkily than it did at home, and I was afraid, ever so slightly, of other bodies veering into mine. It was a type of hyperarousal, I suppose, and it wasn't all that pleasant.

The prospect of the beach now seemed borderline unsafe. Exercising with a single friend, while practising social distancing, was permissible, but it still wasn't clear how far from your home you were allowed to do these things. Not only was I afraid of being on the wrong side of the law, but I was also wary of other people — not so much of their possible germs as of their unpredictability.

Nika was waiting in her car for me and it felt petty not to hug her. In this new pandemic world, our friendship had become stilted, as though we were keeping things from each other, as though we suddenly had secrets. We made our way down onto the sand, and joined the safely distanced lines of beach-walkers in the sun. I liked to walk right at the edge of the sand and the sea, and let the waves wash over my feet. The water was warmer than I expected, barely even refreshing.

At Nika's suggestion I donned a hat against the glare. We'd ambled along the sand for ten minutes or so, when the light shifted abruptly. I took off my hat, I took off my sunglasses. Now the beach was in shade, the light utterly changed, everything softly, radiantly purple. I had experienced it before, a quick shift in afternoon light, but in that moment it felt new. I stared at the sky and the horizon and the water, and the reflection of the sky in the water at my feet.

'The light!' I gasped.

'Yes,' Nika sighed. 'It's very pretty.'

As we trudged on, the sky turned more luminous, shifting through a spectrum of colours. I was mesmerised. I turned to look over my shoulder, trying to take in the entire vista. Nika seemed unperturbed, but I was in awe. We turned around and began the walk back, debating whether it was too dark to swim.

'The water needs to be transparent,' Nika said, 'for me to feel safe going in.'

There had been a spate of shark attacks in recent years, so it was reasonable to be frightened of the dusky waves. In the evening light, they certainly weren't transparent. These waves were opaque, mysterious, tinged with deep violet. Possibly sharky.

I was going in.

Nika stood in the shallows while I waded out. I ducked under the first wave and bobbed in the surf for a while, diving beneath the waves that broke, rising over those that didn't, feeling part of that violet hue. I looked at the sky and I looked at the water and I looked at my arms in that strange evening light. How wild we all are, I thought. All these shimmering atoms.

'You're so brave,' Nika called as I scrambled from the surf towards her.

Brave, I thought, squeezing droplets from my hair in the shallows. Maybe that was all we needed to be?

~

It was five years since my son had brought home the pup. When I threw sticks for him now, he leapt in graceful arcs, catching them effortlessly, glancing nonchalantly over his shoulder to check I'd seen. I thought about how skilled he'd become, of how incremental this process had been. I hoped what I'd done with the older man — moving so awkwardly towards the things I'd desired, never quite catching the stick — had given me practice. In time, maybe I could be graceful in love?

~

The catastrophic pre-pandemic flood had emptied all the debris from the waterhole. The mangled shipping container was still there, but all the sticks and gravel and dirt and leaves had been washed downstream.

When I was a child, the yearly floods would always change the interior of the waterhole. Sometimes they would clear it out and other times they would fill it in. We never worried if one flood made the waterhole less swimmable, as we knew that it would be altered the next time the big rains came. For the last decade that pattern had ceased. Each flood now just brought new debris, filling the waterhole in. The flood that had taken the little house had seemed like the final straw: so much debris, it had created an island where there used to be deep water.

When the coral tree capsized across the whole sorry mess we had not removed it. But with the post-fire flood, the fallen tree had redirected the raging torrents. The water changed its course, and the island of debris was gone. We hadn't realised that the fallen tree was in fact a beginning. We'd thought the waterhole was lost to us, but the old creekscape had returned. A small miracle. Not everything that is destroyed remains so.

~

Everything in the forest is the forest. Systems of care, systems of connection and community. Like the roots of the trees, intertwining. Tending nature, we are tending ourselves. The neighbour's cows got in and trampled my flower garden. It looked wrecked, but in the days that followed, some of those plants, miraculously resilient, began to reshoot. The virus showed us how quickly we could change. Whole ways of being interrupted and altered in a matter of weeks. Nature showed us that, with the smallest amount of breathing room, it was poised for repair. In my homeplace sudden swarms of butterflies appeared, more than we had ever seen. Look what happens when we give other beings some space to inhabit! Thousands of flock pigeons gathered in the trees, taking off in whooshes so thunderous I felt the vibrations of their flight in my chest. Our leaders had told us change was impossible. The virus showed us: we could change course.

~

The pandemic stretched on, different states in different lockdowns; outbreaks flaring up, shutting down cities and travel and the lives we had led before. Autumn, winter, spring, summer. And repeat. If my lover had not broken off with me, we might have been separated for just as long by the circumstances of these unprecedented times. Interstate romance was far less feasible during a pandemic. I worried about him in his unreachable city. How could I know he was truly okay? Sometimes I panicked and called, the panic of not-knowing-he-was-alive overcoming my phone phobia.

'Jessie, you don't have to worry about me,' he'd say, his voice tinged with sadness. I couldn't tell if the sadness was for me or for both of us.

'Okay,' I'd nod, momentarily soothed. 'Okay.'

~

It was lovely, he had said. But there had been nothing of deep feeling between us. I was still grappling with his meaning.

~

When my father left me, dying by suicide, there was no option for repair. He was no longer here — any pain I experienced could not be worked through together. From the moment I heard the news I knew there was a tear in the fabric of my life that could never be restored. The estrangement from the older man echoed this earlier estrangement in ways that amplified the pain. All my old feelings rising. I wanted the older man to do what my father couldn't. Resurrect himself. Reach out. Restore. As though an end to this current estrangement might help ease the rekindled pain from that earlier loss. I understood that we could never go back to the way things were, but the older man wasn't dead. The loss of him wasn't final. It calmed me to imagine him, in his own house, going about his days.

~

Our relationship had been built on distance and longing. Talking with a friend, I'd once proclaimed that the older man was nothing like my father.

'Except in one way,' she said wisely. 'He isn't really here.'

I laughed, discomforted. 'I get to miss him too.' The familiarity of that yearning was hard to ignore.

Now it was truly over, missing him was a difficult habit to break.

~

Each person involved in a romantic relationship creates meaning from their experience. The story that emerges, like all life stories, is an imaginative one, built around the real. In harmonious partnerships, is each imaginative vision just more closely aligned? Experiences I'd held to be meaningful — moments of reciprocated tenderness, connection and love — were not, it turned out, meaningful to the older man. Or not meaningful in the same way. That doesn't mean they didn't happen. Radical self-trust involves allowing your own felt-sense to stand. His narrative didn't have to obliterate mine.

'I thought it was a love story,' I said to a writer friend. Disgruntled, despairing.

'But can't you see,' she said gently, 'it still is.'

~

I think of myself, cascading silver hair that I grew out for him, so he wouldn't feel so old. Naked and kneeling on his bed, open-faced, reaching out to touch him, not knowing that his love had already faded, still giving what I had. That memory used to fill me with so much shame. To have been so trusting in the midst of betrayal. To have so falsely believed. But now I just think of my own sweetness, the taste of me still fresh and tangy, desire pulsing heavily through my veins. How brave I was, I think. How brave I can be.

waterhole

To get to the waterhole, I tread through the rainforest. Down a slope, on steps carved from the dirt by my father's hands. At the base I follow a worn path. The trees are mammoth. All around me seedlings burst through the soil, reaching for the light. The path curves and the expanse of the waterhole comes into view. At dusk it is shadowy, mysterious, the surrounding boulders luminous in the disappearing light. The pebbly soil of the creek bank gives way under my feet. I pause at the threshold, sinking into the land. Stepping in, my legs tingle. Goosebumps rise up my thighs. My body is thrumming. I drop my hands into the water and it seems to rise up to meet me. The waterhole hasn't been this deep in decades. I never thought it would be this deep again. I duck my head under and surrender to the darkness. Beneath the surface I am caressed, I am held. Coming up for air, I stare at the moon through the canopy. There are no fireflies, but they were here in spring, so I know we haven't lost them yet.

This world I love, holding all our destruction.

May I mend whatever it is I have wrecked.

May I give as much as I take.

Floating there, all gravity disappears. The water sluices at my ears, I feel its silver touch. In the waterhole, I am buoyant, all pain erased. When I stand, the water runs off me in rivulets, light, electric. Crouching in the shallows, I dip my hands under the water, returning the touch.

further reading

Abram, David, *Becoming Animal: An Earthy Cosmology*, Random House, 2011

Brown, Daniel P., et al., *Attachment Disturbances in Adults: Treatment for Comprehensive Repair*, W. W. Norton & Company Inc, 2016

Herman, Judith, *Trauma and Recovery: The Aftermath of Violence — From Domestic Abuse to Political Terror*, Basic Books, 1992

Karen, Robert, *Becoming Attached: First Relationships and How They Shape Our Capacity to Love*, Oxford University Press, 1998

Learner, Harriet, *The Dance of Intimacy: A Woman's Guide to Courageous Acts of Change in Key Relationships*, Harper & Row, 1989

Levine, Amir, and Rachel S.F. Heller, *Attached: The New Science of Adult Attachment and How It Can Help You Find — And Keep — Love*, Tarcher/Penguin, 2011

Lukas, Christopher, and Henry M. Seiden, *Silent Grief: Living in the Wake of Suicide (Revised Edition)*, Jessica Kingsley, 2007

Nagoski, Emily, *Come as You Are: The Surprising New Science That Will Transform Your Sex Life*, Scribe Publications, 2015

Perel, Esther, *Mating in Captivity: Unlocking Erotic Intelligence*, Harper Paperbacks, 2007

Perel, Esther, *State of Affairs: Rethinking Infidelity*, Yellow Kite, 2019

Saltman, Bethany, *Strange Situation: A Mother's Journey into the Science of Attachment*, Scribe Publications, 2020

Van der Kolk, Bessel, *The Body Keeps the Score: Mind, Brain and Body in the Transformation of Trauma*, Penguin, 2014

Wohlleben, Peter, *The Hidden Life of Trees: What They Feel, How They Communicate*, Black Inc, 2016

acknowledgements

Desire was written in close to real time — I wrote about my experiences while living them, without the benefit of hindsight. It's so tempting to see our lives as having a specific linear narrative, but while in the midst of life, these narratives can seem (or be) far less clear. I wanted my work to reflect this uncertainty. Our experiences, and our responses to them, are unknowable in advance, as are the experiences and responses of other people we're relating to. This might seem an obvious truth, but it's a terrifying, highwire way to write a memoir.

I am indebted to the writers experimenting with fragmentary narratives who came before me, especially Sarah Sentilles and Maggie Nelson, whose dazzling works I wrote my master's thesis on.

I want to acknowledge Maria Tumarkin and her two intriguing essays 'This Narrated Life' and 'Wildness: Feminism, Identity, and the Willingness to be Defeated', which spoke directly to the troubles I had bringing this work into being. You shone a torch, lighting up the road ahead.

Shout out, also, to all the queer authors writing so exquisitely about desire and sex. I have always been inspired by the openness and intensity you bring to your work. Thank you for being my guides.

For those interested, the 500-page tome on attachment theory that I refer to is Robert Karen's *Becoming Attached: First Relationships and How They Shape Our Capacity to Love*. The phrase 'Everything in the forest is the forest' is plucked from Richard Powers' incredible novel *The Overstory*. I am thankful for the wisdom embedded in both these works.

Enormous thanks to Varuna, the National Writers' House, who continue to offer the Australian writing community a valuable space in which to connect.

I am grateful to my earliest readers: Lisa Walker, Bronwyn Birdsall, Louise Nicholls and Danika Cottrell. Your sensitive, careful feedback was so sustaining. Many thanks also to my supervisors, Professor Bronwyn Lea and Dr Karin Sellberg, who had many helpful insights.

For much-needed writerly chats and comradery, thanks to Helen Burns, Siboney Saavedra, Michelle Taylor, Kayte Nunn, Hayley Katzen, Therese Spruhan, Romy Ash, Anna Krien, Bradley McCann, James Murray, Eliza Henry-Jones, Carrie Tiffany, Jane Rawson, Josephine Browne, Emily Brugman, Gretchen Miller, Anna Finnane, Penny Nelson, Jennifer Hauptman, Meg Bignell, Maggie Mackellar and Carolyn Fraser. Big thanks to Jane Camens, who generously opened her home to me in the earliest stages of writing this book. Much gratitude, also, for Marlene Farry, Amanda Patterson, Joy Ross and Melanie Manton.

Huge appreciation for Jenny Darling, my agent, whose unanticipated enthusiasm for this book gave me such courage. I am terrified of you and buoyed by you in equal measure.

To Penny Hueston and Michael Heyward, and the whole team at Text Publishing, thank you for your faith in this work, and for the exceptional care you took with my words.

Special thanks to Mike and Judy Nicholls, and the Nicholls clan, for the welcome you extended to this ring-in, and for modelling for us all such enduring love and care. May Pete live always in our hearts.

So much love for my friends and family, who held me so well during the writing and editing process. I hope I give as much as I take.

Finally, to all those who appear in the text, anonymously or not, thank you for sharing your lives with me. May we be selves always becoming, our histories intertwined like the roots of the trees.